2—

What's for Dinner?

Over 200 Delicious Recipes That Work Every Time

BY MARYANA VOLLSTEDT

CHRONICLE BOOKS
SAN FRANCISCO

Library of Congress Cataloging-in-Publication Data:

Vollstedt, Maryana.
What's for dinner: Over 200 delicious recipes that work every time
by Maryana Vollstedt

p. cm.
Includes Index.
ISBN 0-8118-1395-9 (pbk.)
1. Dinners and dining. 2. Cookery. 3. Menus. I. Title
TX737.V65 1997
641.5'55—dc21
96-37107 CIP

Printed in the United States of America.

Cover and Book Design by Friedrich Design/SF
Pete Friedrich & Knut Ettling

Illustrations by Mary Lynn Blasutta
Headline typeface is "Pila," designed by Pete Friedrich

Distributed in Canada by Raincoast Books
9050 Shaughnessy Street
Vancouver, British Columbia V6P 6E5

10 9 8 7 6 5 4 3

Chronicle Books LLC
85 Second Street
San Francisco, California 94105

www.chroniclebooks.com

Dedication

This book is dedicated to my patient husband, Reed, chief tester, consultant, and computer person.

And to my grown children, Julie, Scott, and Gregg, who are also good cooks, and Jon, who never did learn to cook but who, when he was a young boy, always came home from school with the same greeting: "Hi, Mom, what's for dinner?"

Acknowledgments

To Bill LeBlond, senior editor at Chronicle Books, for his faith that I could produce another popular and practical book.

To Frances Bowles, for her expert copyediting and helpful suggestions for this book.

To Jim Herbold, friend and computer consultant.

To all my friends, who helped critique my recipes and who would willingly come for a casual testing dinner on the spur of the moment.

Contents

Introduction

Written for busy people who expect good results with a minimum amount of time in the kitchen, these recipes include tempting hors d'oeuvres, satisfying soups, creative salads, terrific entrées, quick pasta and grain dishes, and desserts that will appeal to the beginner as well as the experienced cook.

Every entrée has menu suggestions; some have helpful hints and other information. The recipes are straightforward and practical with complete, easy-to-follow directions that make cooking fun and easy.

Most ingredients are readily available and fresh ingredients are used whenever possible. Today's cooks are more health conscious and aware of good nutrition, so reduced cholesterol, fat, and calories are taken into consideration.

This is a cookbook that will soon become your favorite.

Great Beginnings

Start the evening in style by serving a delicious hors d'oeuvre or appetizer as a prelude to dinner. Your guests will appreciate something to nibble on, especially if wine or drinks are being served. Before a meal, hors d'oeuvres should tempt the taste buds, not dull the appetite. The best rule is to keep the cocktail hour short and the hors d'oeuvres simple.

Hors d'Oeuvre and Appetizer Basics

For an open house, hors d'oeuvres are heartier and, depending on time of day, often serve as a meal. Offer a variety of complementary hors d'oeuvres; hot, cold, hearty, and low-calorie should be offered.

Select recipes that can be made ahead so that you can enjoy your party.

Be sure that hot hors d'oeuvres are hot and cold ones cold.

Provide small plates and napkins.

Arrange the hors d'oeuvres attractively on a large table or in different locations about the house to promote mingling and socializing.

Replenish the food trays often to keep them looking fresh and appealing.

Bread with Cream Cheese and Pesto Spread

Easy to make, this hearty hors d'oeuvre is tasty as well as colorful and useful when you are short of time. Use purchased pesto or make your own.

1 package (3 ounces) cream cheese, softened

2 cloves garlic, minced

1 loaf French bread, split lengthwise

1/2 cup Basil Pesto (page 193), or purchased pesto (see note)

2 tomatoes, seeded, chopped, and drained

Freshly grated Parmesan cheese

Preheat oven to 350°F. In a bowl combine cream cheese and garlic. Spread on cut side of bread. Spread pesto on top. Add tomatoes and Parmesan cheese.

Place on a baking sheet and bake until bread is warmed and cheese is melted, about 10 minutes. Cut into serving pieces and serve immediately.

Note: If using purchased pesto, pour off some of the oil that accumulates on the top, then stir to blend before spreading on bread.

Antipasto Platter

Antipasto is an Italian word for an appetizer served before the meal. Generally, it is an assortment of vegetables, meats, fish, and cheeses arranged on a platter or tray. It can be served as an hors d'oeuvre or as the first course. Use the following suggestions to create your own antipasto platter.

1 small head cauliflower, broken into florets

1/2 pound fresh green beans

1/2 pound whole mushrooms

2 red bell peppers, roasted (page 8) and cut into strips

Italian Dressing (page 56)

Greens for lining the platter, such as Swiss chard, romaine lettuce, or leaf lettuce

MEATS AND FISH
(CHOOSE 2 OR 3)

3 ounces dry salami, sliced

3 ounces pepperoni, sliced

3 ounces prosciutto, thinly sliced and rolled

1 cup cooked fresh tuna, or 1 can (7 1/2 ounces) tuna, drained

1 tin (2 ounces) anchovy fillets, drained

To prepare vegetables, place cauliflower on steamer rack over gently boiling water, cover, and steam 7 minutes. Drain under cold water and set aside. Repeat with beans, steam for 5 or 6 minutes, and drain under cold water. Marinate all vegetables, including peppers, separately in Italian Dressing for several hours in refrigerator.

CHEESES
(CHOOSE 1 OR 2)

4 ounces provolone
  cheese, thinly sliced
  and rolled
4 ounces mozzarella
  cheese, thinly sliced
  and rolled
4 ounces goat cheese, cut
  into 1/2-inch cubes

OTHER ADDITIONS

1 can (15 ounces)
  garbanzo beans,
  drained and rinsed,
  and marinated in
  Italian Dressing
1 jar (6 ounces)
  marinated artichoke
  hearts, drained
2 hard-cooked eggs, cut
  into wedges
1 cup well-drained ripe
  olives
1 bunch green onions
2 tablespoons well-
  drained capers

To assemble, line a large tray or platter with lettuce leaves. With a slotted spoon arrange drained vegetables in groups on leaves. Add meats, fish, cheeses, garbanzo beans, and artichoke hearts in mounds. Garnish with eggs, olives, and onions and sprinkle with capers.

Serve extra dressing if desired.

Sun-dried Tomato Pesto on Crostini

This delicious pesto has many uses. Spread on crostini or sourdough bread as an appetizer or mix with cooked pasta for a side dish. It is also good as a topping on grilled polenta.

¾ cup packed, cut-up, dry sun-dried tomatoes (not in oil)
1 cup boiling water
¼ cup freshly grated Parmesan cheese
5 large basil leaves
2 parsley sprigs
2 tablespoons pine nuts
2 cloves garlic, cut up
3 tablespoons olive oil
12 to 14 Basic Crostini (recipe follows)

In a small bowl soak sun-dried tomatoes in boiling water for 10 minutes to reconstitute them. Drain. In a food processor combine sun-dried tomatoes, Parmesan cheese, basil, parsley, pine nuts, and garlic and blend briefly. Slowly add oil and process until a smooth paste forms. Stop motor and scrape down sides of bowl, if necessary.

If making ahead, cover, and refrigerate. Bring to room temperature before using. Serve on crostini.

Basic Crostini

Crostini are simply bread rounds toasted and used as a base for top-pings. They may be served as an hors d'oeuvre or with soup or salad.

1/4 cup olive oil
2 large cloves garlic, quartered
1 baguette, cut into slices 1/4- to 1/3-inch thick

In a small jar combine oil and garlic. Let stand to absorb flavors, about 30 minutes.

Preheat broiler. Arrange bread slices on baking sheet and broil on first side until lightly browned, about 3 minutes. Turn slices over and brush with garlic oil. Broil 1 to 2 minutes longer.

Makes about 30 to 35 slices

Note: The bread slices may be baked instead of broiled. Arrange bread slices on baking sheet and place in a preheated 350°F oven. Brush one side with garlic oil. Bake until lightly browned and crisp, about 10 minutes.

Roasted Red Bell Pepper Crostini with Feta Cheese

This hors d'oeuvre makes a nice introduction to a company dinner. Allow two to three crostini per person.

1½ cups chopped
  Marinated Roasted
  Red Bell Peppers
  (recipe follows)
20 to 24 Crostini
  (page 7)
3 ounces feta cheese,
  crumbled

Place about 1 tablespoon marinated peppers on each slice of toast. Sprinkle with feta cheese. Serve immediately.

Marinated Roasted Red Bell Peppers

2 roasted red bell peppers
  (see note), chopped,
  or one 7½-ounce jar
  (1½ cups) purchased
  roasted red peppers,
  drained and chopped
1 tablespoon olive oil
1 or 2 cloves garlic,
  minced
1 tablespoon red wine
  vinegar
Dash of salt

In a small bowl mix all ingredients together. Cover and chill several hours.

Makes about 1½ cups

Note: To roast red bell peppers, preheat broiler. Cut pepper in half lengthwise and remove stems, seeds, and ribs. At 2-inch intervals, make a 1-inch slash around the edge of each half pepper. Place skin-side up on a foil-lined baking sheet with a rim and press peppers down to flatten. Broil until skin is charred, about 10 minutes. Transfer peppers to a paper bag or covered bowl. Let stand 15 minutes. Remove peppers and peel off skin.

Warm Brie with Marinated Roasted Red Peppers and Roasted Garlic

SERVES 6

Serve this impressive hors d'oeuvre as a first course on individual plates with warm baguette slices. Provide small knives for spreading.

1 Brie wedge
(10 to 12 ounces)
Marinated Roasted Red
Peppers (page 8), cut
into strips and drained
2 to 3 tablespoons
drained capers
Roasted Garlic
(recipe follows)
Curly-leaf lettuce for
lining plates

Preheat oven to 325°F. Place Brie on a pie plate and place in oven until warmed, 6 to 7 minutes (do not allow to get runny). Divide Brie evenly onto 6 small, lettuce-lined plates. Top with red pepper mixture. Sprinkle with capers. Place several roasted garlic cloves on the side and 2 or 3 bread slices around the edge.

Roasted Garlic

Roasted garlic can be used in whipped potatoes, on vegetables and pizza, with pasta, or spread on bread.

4 large garlic heads
2 teaspoons olive oil

Preheat oven to 400°F. Remove outer, papery skin of garlic head but do not peel or separate cloves. With a knife slice ¼ inch off the top, leaving the head intact. Place each head on a square of heavy-duty aluminum foil. Drizzle ½ teaspoon oil over each head. Fold foil over garlic and seal tightly. Bake until garlic is very soft, about 45 minutes. Let cool. Slip cloves out of skin and set aside.

Serves 6

Party Cheese Ball

MAKES ONE 3-INCH BALL

Red and green flecks make this creamy cheese ball a perfect hors d'oeuvre for the holidays. Horseradish is the secret ingredient, adding extra zest. Serve with crackers or crudités (raw vegetables).

1 package (8 ounces) light cream cheese, at room temperature

1 tablespoon prepared cream-style horseradish

1/2 cup freshly grated Parmesan cheese

1/4 cup drained pimiento-stuffed green olives plus 1 tablespoon of the brine

Red chard or red cabbage leaves, for lining plate

4 pimiento-stuffed green olives, sliced, for garnish

Place cream cheese, horseradish, Parmesan cheese, whole olives, and brine in a food processor and blend until smooth. Scrape down sides of bowl with a spatula if necessary.

Transfer to a piece of plastic wrap and shape into a ball. Wrap and chill several hours.

To serve, place in the center of a large plate lined with chard or cabbage leaves. Decorate the ball with sliced olives. Surround with crackers and strips of vegetables. Serve at room temperature.

Beer Cheese Spread

Four cheeses are combined with beer to make this mellow cheese spread. Make at least a day in advance to allow the flavors to develop. Serve with crackers or toast rounds. It will keep in the refrigerator for several weeks.

2 cups grated Cheddar cheese

1 cup grated Monterey Jack cheese

2 ounces cream cheese, cut up

1/4 cup freshly grated Parmesan cheese

2 cloves garlic, cut up

1/2 teaspoon dry mustard

2 drops Tabasco sauce

1 teaspoon Worcestershire sauce

1/2 cup beer, allowed to go flat

In a food processor combine all ingredients and process until blended. Pack into a bowl or crock, cover, and refrigerate overnight. Will keep up to 2 weeks.

Serve at room temperature for easy spreading.

Quesadillas

An easy hors d'oeuvre to serve with drinks. For a main course, add cooked chicken, avocado, salsa, olives, refried beans, green chiles, or chopped green onions.

4 large flour tortillas
2 cups grated Monterey Jack cheese
Vegetable oil, for brushing skillet
Fresh Tomato Salsa (page 13), or prepared salsa

Lay tortillas on a flat surface and sprinkle ½ cup cheese on half of each tortilla. Fold over into a semicircle. Brush a non-stick skillet lightly with oil and place on medium-high heat. Cook one quesadilla at a time until lightly browned and cheese is melted, about 2 minutes on each side.

Keep warm in a warm oven or cover with foil until all quesadillas are cooked. Brush skillet with more oil if needed. Cut each quesadilla in quarters and serve immediately with salsa.

Fresh Tomato Salsa

MAKES ABOUT 2 ½ CUPS

Salsa appears on the Mexican table at every meal, to be served with almost any dish. You can make it as hot as you like by varying the amount and variety of chiles you use. It is best when made fresh.

2 cups coarsely chopped tomatoes, seeded and drained

2 or 3 jalapeño chiles, ribs and seeds removed and finely chopped (see note)

½ cup finely chopped white onion

1 tablespoon lime or lemon juice

1 to 2 tablespoons chopped cilantro or parsley

Salt and freshly ground pepper to taste

In a small bowl mix together all ingredients. Serve immediately.

Note: When working with chiles, wear gloves or wash hands thoroughly afterward.

Broiled Shrimp Rounds

Small cooked shrimp are always available and lend themselves to this easy hors d'oeuvre that goes together in just minutes. This also makes a good open-face sandwich on an English muffin.

1 package (3 ounces)
  cream cheese, softened
1 tablespoon mayonnaise
2 teaspoons lemon juice
1 teaspoon paprika
1/4 teaspoon dry mustard
1/8 teaspoon salt
1 cup chopped, cooked,
  small shrimp
Baguette or cocktail rye
  bread slices, about 20

Prepare broiler. In a bowl stir together all ingredients except shrimp and bread. Fold in shrimp.

Place bread on a baking sheet. Broil one side until lightly toasted, about 40 seconds. Remove pan from oven and turn bread over. Spread on shrimp mixture and broil until bubbly, 2 to 3 minutes.

Shrimp Salsa

A great introduction to a Mexican dinner party. Serve with tortilla chips and provide napkins or small plates.

½ pound small, cooked shrimp

1 cup prepared salsa, briefly drained

2 tablespoons catsup

1 tablespoon lime or lemon juice

1 large avocado, peeled and cut into bite-sized pieces

3 green onions including some tender green tops, sliced

1 small tomato, seeded, chopped, and drained

1 or 2 tablespoons chopped fresh cilantro or parsley

In a bowl stir together all ingredients. Cover and refrigerate several hours before serving.

Hot Shrimp Hors d'Oeuvre

Serve this shrimp in a chafing dish along with Spicy Red Sauce for dipping. Make the sauce several hours ahead.

¼ cup butter or
   margarine
1 pound large shrimp,
   peeled and deveined,
   with tails intact
2 cloves garlic, minced
1 teaspoon dried dill
Salt to taste
½ cup dry white wine
Spicy Red Sauce
   (recipe follows)

In a skillet over medium heat, melt butter. Add shrimp, garlic, and dill and cook, turning several times, until shrimp turn pink, about 2 minutes. Season with salt, add wine, and cook 1 minute on low heat. Transfer to a chafing dish to keep warm. Serve with Spicy Red Sauce.

Spicy Red Sauce

¾ cup catsup
¼ cup bottled chili sauce
2 teaspoons prepared
   horseradish, or to taste
¼ teaspoon cayenne
   pepper
1 teaspoon fresh lemon
   juice
1 teaspoon Worcestershire
   sauce

In a small bowl stir together all ingredients. Cover and refrigerate several hours before serving to blend flavors. Serve at room temperature.

Makes about 1 cup

Crab-filled Mushrooms

Stuffed mushrooms are always a party favorite, especially when they are filled with fresh, delicate Dungeness crab. Using the food processor saves time in chopping.

1 pound (about 20) medium mushrooms of equal size

2 green onions including some tender green tops, cut up

1 clove garlic, cut up

2 tablespoons butter or margarine

1/4 cup dry bread crumbs

1/4 pound fresh crab meat, flaked

2 teaspoons fresh lemon juice

1/4 teaspoon salt

Vegetable oil, for brushing on mushroom caps

Paprika

Clean mushrooms and remove stems neatly. Place stems in food processor along with 1 mushroom cap, green onions, and garlic. Process until coarsely chopped.

Preheat oven to 350°F. In a small, nonstick skillet over medium heat melt butter. Add mushroom mixture and sauté until vegetables are soft, about 1 minute. Remove from heat and add crumbs, crab, lemon juice, and salt and mix well. Rub oil on sides and bottom of caps. Fill mushroom caps with filling, making a round mound on top. Sprinkle with paprika.

Place on a baking sheet and bake until mushrooms are heated through and slightly soft, about 10 minutes. Transfer to a plate and serve immediately.

Crab for Crackers

Arrange assorted crackers around a bowl filled with this delicious crab mixture. It can also be served on a bed of lettuce for a salad.

½ pound Dungeness crab, sorted and flaked

1 egg, hard-cooked and chopped

2 green onions including some tender green tops, sliced

3 tablespoons light mayonnaise

1 tablespoon chili sauce

1 tablespoon capers, drained (optional)

1 teaspoon lemon juice

2 drops Tabasco sauce

In a bowl stir together all ingredients. Serve with crackers and provide a knife for spreading. Add more mayonnaise if necessary.

Variation: Omit egg and add ¼ pound small, cooked shrimp, chopped. Add more mayonnaise if necessary.

Smoked Salmon Spread

Smoked salmon is a delicacy that makes a tempting hors d'oeuvre. Serve plain or blended with cream cheese as a spread to serve with jícama slices or crackers. Make ahead so the flavors can blend.

4 ounces smoked salmon, flaked

1 package (3 ounces) cream cheese, cut up, at room temperature

1 tablespoon light mayonnaise

1 teaspoon lemon juice

1/2 teaspoon dill weed (optional)

2 parsley sprigs

Lettuce leaves, for lining platter

Slices of jícama or crackers

Place all ingredients except jícama, crackers, and lettuce in food processor. Process until well blended. Place in small bowl, cover, and refrigerate several hours.

To serve, lay lettuce leaves on a platter. Mound salmon mixture in the center. Arrange jícama or crackers around the salmon. Serve immediately.

Party Salmon Mousse

This appealing hors d'oeuvre is good for a large party because it can be made ahead and yields a lot. Serve with crackers and provide a knife for spreading.

1 envelope unflavored gelatin
1/4 cup water
2 cups cooked fresh salmon, flaked, or 1 can (16 ounces) salmon, drained, skin and dark flesh removed
2 green onions including some tender green tops, cut up
2 sprigs parsley
2 teaspoons snipped fresh dill, or 1/2 teaspoon dill weed
1 tablespoon fresh lemon juice
1/2 teaspoon salt
1 teaspoon paprika
1/4 teaspoon Worcestershire sauce
2 tablespoons mayonnaise
1 cup light sour cream
Parsley sprigs, for garnish

In a small bowl stir gelatin into water. Place bowl in pan of water over medium heat, stirring until gelatin dissolves, about 2 minutes. Set aside.

Place all remaining ingredients (except sour cream) in a food processor and process until smooth. Transfer to a bowl and fold in sour cream and gelatin. Cover and refrigerate several hours or overnight. Serve garnished with parsley.

Sun-dried Tomato and Feta Cheese Dip

Creamy feta cheese is blended with sun-dried tomatoes for a colorful, delicious dip. Serve with toast rounds or crackers.

3 tablespoons dry sun-dried tomatoes (not packed in oil)

1 cup boiling water

3 ounces mild feta cheese, at room temperature

4 ounces cream cheese, at room temperature, cut up

2 cloves garlic, cut up

$1/4$ teaspoon dried thyme, crumbled

1 tablespoon red wine vinegar

3 sprigs parsley

In a small bowl soak sun-dried tomatoes in boiling water for 10 minutes, then drain and dry. Place all ingredients in food processor or blender and process until smooth. Transfer to a small bowl, cover, and refrigerate several hours or overnight. Bring to room temperature before serving.

Curried Seafood

MAKES 2 CUPS

Start the party with this savory seafood spread. Provide a knife for spreading on crackers.

1 package (8 ounces) cream cheese, cut up

1 tablespoon freshly grated Parmesan cheese

1 tablespoon milk

1 tablespoon mayonnaise

1 clove garlic, minced

1/4 teaspoon curry powder

1 teaspoon Worcestershire sauce

1 tablespoon lemon juice

4 ounces fresh crab, flaked

4 ounces small shrimp, chopped

1/4 cup finely chopped celery

In food processor blend cheeses, milk, mayonnaise, garlic, curry powder, Worcestershire sauce, and lemon juice. Fold in crab, shrimp, and celery. Transfer to a serving dish.

Baked Black Bean Dip

Black beans have become popular over the past few years because they are nutritious as well as delicious. They can be served in many ways. Here they are incorporated into a colorful dip. Serve with large tortilla chips.

1 can (16 ounces) black beans, rinsed and drained

1/4 cup light sour cream

1 clove garlic, cut up

2 tablespoons diced chiles

1/4 teaspoon ground cumin

1 cup grated Cheddar cheese

8 green onions including some tender green tops, sliced

1/2 cup sliced black olives

1 small tomato, seeded, chopped, and drained

Preheat oven to 400°F. Place beans, sour cream, garlic, chiles, and cumin in food processor or blender. Process briefly with on-off pulses until mixed, but still chunky. Spread mixture in a 9-inch glass pie plate. Top with cheese, onions, olives, and tomato.

Bake until heated through and cheese is melted, about 15 minutes, or microwave, 2 to 3 minutes.

Chunky Guacamole

This zesty dip served with tortilla chips is a natural starter to a Mexican dinner. It is also served as an accompaniment to other Mexican foods such as enchiladas and tacos.

3 or 4 ripe avocados, halved and pits removed

1 small tomato, seeded, chopped, and drained

2 tablespoons fresh lemon juice

1 clove garlic, minced

1 teaspoon Worcestershire sauce

½ teaspoon salt

⅛ teaspoon cayenne pepper

1 to 2 drops Tabasco sauce

4 green onions including some tender green tops, chopped

2 tablespoons chopped olives, drained

With a spoon, scoop the avocado pulp into a bowl and mash with a fork. Stir in remaining ingredients and mix well. Cover and refrigerate several hours.

Note: If a smooth dip is desired, process avocados, lemon juice, and seasonings in a food processor or blender. Fold in tomato and olives and top with onions.

Hummus

A Middle Eastern dip or spread, hummus is easily made in a food processor or blender. Serve with Pocket Bread Wedges as an introduction to a lamb entrée.

1 can (15½ ounces)
    garbanzo beans, rinsed
    and drained
¼ cup tahini (see note)
1 tablespoon lemon juice
2 tablespoons olive oil
2 cloves garlic, cut up
¼ teaspoon salt
1 teaspoon ground cumin
¼ teaspoon freshly
    ground pepper
Pocket Bread Wedges
    (recipe follows)

Combine all ingredients except pocket bread in food processor or blender and process until smooth, stopping and scraping the sides down if necessary. Cover and chill.

Note: Tahini (sesame seed paste) is available at specialty food stores and some supermarkets.

Pocket Bread Wedges

¼ cup olive oil
2 cloves garlic, sliced
3 pocket breads

In a small bowl mix olive oil and garlic and let stand 30 minutes.

Preheat oven to 300°F. Halve pocket bread and cut each half into 4 wedges. Open wedges, split them into triangles and place, smooth-side down, on a baking sheet. Brush with garlic oil and bake until slightly browned, about 10 minutes.

Makes 48 wedges

Black Bean Nachos

Serve this hearty snack with margaritas as an introduction to a Mexican dinner.

1 can (15 ounces) black beans, rinsed and drained

1/3 cup homemade or prepared salsa

1 small tomato, seeded, chopped, and drained

4 green onions including some tender green tops, chopped

1 1/2 cups grated Monterey Jack cheese

1/4 cup ripe olives, sliced

4 tablespoons sour cream (optional)

Tortilla chips, warmed

Dry black beans on a paper towel. Spread beans on a pie plate or decorative oven-proof dish.

Preheat oven to 425°F. In a small bowl stir together salsa, tomato, and onions. Spread evenly over beans. Sprinkle with cheese. Add olives and bake until warmed thoroughly and cheese is melted, 5 to 6 minutes. Add 4 dollops of sour cream around the edge of beans. Serve immediately with tortilla chips.

Blue Cheese Meatballs

These meatballs have a unique flavor and make a great hors d'oeuvre. Serve with toothpicks for spearing.

1 pound lean ground beef

1 tablespoon finely chopped onion

4 ounces blue cheese, crumbled

1 clove garlic, minced

1 teaspoon Worcestershire sauce

$1/3$ cup dry bread crumbs

$1/4$ teaspoon dried thyme, crumbled

$1/4$ teaspoon dried rosemary, crumbled

2 tablespoons chopped parsley

$1/2$ cup milk

$1/4$ cup dry red wine (optional)

Preheat oven to 375°F. In a bowl mix all ingredients except wine thoroughly. Form into $1/2$-inch balls. Place on a baking sheet with a rim and bake until browned, about 10 minutes. Serve immediately or keep warm by placing over heat in a chafing dish with wine.

Note: Made larger, these meatballs can also be served as a main course: Form into 1-inch balls.

Soup
The Original Comfort Food

*What is more welcome than a hearty bowl of soup
on a cold winter night or a chilled soup on a hot summer day?
Soups serve many purposes, from an introduction to a meal to
a complete, "stick-to-the-ribs" meal in a bowl. With little
effort, homemade soups can be enjoyed often.
Most soups take less than an hour to make
and are far superior in flavor and nutrition
to the canned or packaged variety. Many
soups can be made in advance and
reheated at serving time. In fact, they
usually improve in flavor when served
the next day. Soups can be creative and
varied according to taste, so add your own personal touch.*

Soup Basics

- Use fresh, top-quality ingredients.

- Allow 1¼ to 1½ cups for a first course and 1½ to 2 cups for a main course.

- Serve hot soups in warmed bowls.

- Reheat soup on low heat as it burns easily.

- Instead of the usual white sauce, creamy soups can be thickened with puréed vegetables prepared in the food processor or blender. Leftover vegetables, puréed and combined with broth, also make good soups.

Cream of Mushroom Soup

Homemade fresh mushroom soup cannot be compared to the canned variety in flavor or texture. The addition of yogurt makes it lighter and creamier.

3 to 4 tablespoons butter
  or margarine
1 cup chopped yellow
  onion
1 pound white
  mushrooms, sliced
1 tablespoon fresh lemon
  juice
1/4 cup all-purpose flour
3 cups chicken broth
1 1/2 cups light cream or
  milk
1/4 teaspoon dried thyme,
  crumbled
3/4 teaspoon salt
Freshly ground pepper
  to taste
Plain nonfat yogurt

In a saucepan melt butter over medium heat. Add onion and sauté 3 minutes. Add mushrooms and lemon juice and sauté until vegetables are soft, about 5 minutes longer. Stir in flour and mix well. Slowly add broth and bring to a boil over high heat, stirring constantly until thickened, about 2 minutes.

Transfer to food processor or blender and purée. Return soup to pan and add cream or milk, thyme, salt, and pepper. Simmer on low heat until flavors are blended, about 5 minutes. Ladle into bowls and swirl about 1 tablespoon yogurt into each bowl. Serve immediately.

Garden–fresh Tomato–Basil Soup

For best results, use garden-fresh, fully ripe tomatoes. Winter tomatoes or canned tomatoes can be used but are not equal in flavor or texture.

3 tablespoons butter or margarine

1/2 cup chopped yellow onion

2 cloves garlic, minced

3 tablespoons flour

2 cups chicken broth

3 pounds (about 8 medium) tomatoes, peeled, seeded, and chopped (see notes)

3 sprigs fresh parsley, chopped

1 teaspoon sugar

1/2 teaspoon salt

1 tablespoon chopped fresh thyme, or 1/4 teaspoon dried thyme, crumbled

1/4 cup chopped fresh basil, or 1 teaspoon dried basil, crumbled

1/4 teaspoon paprika

1 bay leaf

Freshly ground pepper to taste

Light sour cream or plain nonfat yogurt, for garnish (optional)

Basil leaf slivers, for garnish (see notes)

In a soup pot over medium heat melt butter. Add onion and garlic and sauté until tender, about 5 minutes. Stir in flour and blend thoroughly. Gradually add broth and stir until bubbly and slightly thickened. Add remaining ingredients, except sour cream and basil. Bring to a boil, reduce heat and simmer, covered, for 30 minutes. Remove bay leaf and discard.

Transfer to food processor or blender and purée until blended. Ladle into bowls and top with a dollop of sour cream and sprinkle with basil. Serve immediately.

Notes:

• To peel tomatoes, drop them in boiling water for 30 seconds.

• To make basil slivers, lay 5 basil leaves, one on top of the other, roll up tightly lengthwise, and slice horizontally.

Potato-Onion Soup

This is a soup that can be made at almost anytime because the ingredients are usually in the pantry.

2 tablespoons butter or margarine

1 cup chopped yellow onion

2 celery stalks, sliced

2 large potatoes, peeled and diced (about 2½ cups)

1 cup chicken broth or water

2 cups milk

¼ cup chopped parsley

¾ teaspoon salt

Freshly ground pepper to taste

3 bacon strips, cooked and crumbled (optional)

Paprika, for sprinkling on top

3 green onions including some tender green tops, sliced (optional)

In a large saucepan over medium heat melt butter. Add onion and celery and sauté until vegetables are slightly soft, about 6 minutes. Add potatoes and chicken broth and bring to a boil. Reduce temperature to low and simmer, covered, until vegetables are soft, about 20 minutes. Remove 1 cup vegetables and set aside.

Transfer remaining soup to food processor or blender and process until smooth. Return to pan and add milk, parsley, and reserved vegetables. Season with salt and pepper and reheat on medium heat about 5 minutes.

Ladle into bowls and sprinkle with bacon or paprika and green onions. Serve immediately.

Peanut Butter, Mushroom, and Broccoli Soup

This unusual combination makes a delicious soup. If you are a peanut butter fan, you'll enjoy every spoonful.

2 quarts chicken broth

Freshly ground pepper to taste

1/3 cup pearl barley, sorted, rinsed, and drained

1 cup chunky-style peanut butter

2 cups chopped fresh broccoli florets, or 1 package (10 ounces) frozen chopped broccoli, thawed and drained

1/2 pound fresh mushrooms, chopped

1 tablespoon fresh lemon juice

Salt, to taste

Combine broth and pepper in a large soup pot. Bring to a boil and add barley. Reduce heat to low, cover, and simmer until barley is tender, about 50 minutes.

Using a wire whisk, blend in peanut butter. Add broccoli, mushrooms, and lemon juice and simmer, covered, over medium-low heat until vegetables are tender, about 15 minutes. Add salt and simmer, uncovered, 5 to 10 minutes. Serve immediately.

Curried Carrot Soup

I adapted this soup from one I was served in an elegant London restaurant. The orange pieces add a surprise taste and texture. Although it can be made at any time of the year, fresh carrots from the garden will impart the best flavor.

4 cups sliced carrots (about 1 1/2 pounds)

1/2 yellow onion, chopped

1 small turnip, chopped (optional)

1 small potato, peeled and quartered

1 cup water

3 cups chicken broth

1 teaspoon salt

1/4 teaspoon fines herbes

1/4 to 1/2 teaspoon curry powder

1/4 teaspoon paprika

1/8 teaspoon white pepper

1 orange, peeled, cut into bite-sized pieces, and drained, for garnish

Light sour cream or plain nonfat yogurt, for topping

In a saucepan combine the carrots, onion, turnip, potato, and water. Bring to a boil over high heat, then cover and simmer over medium-low heat until vegetables are tender, about 30 minutes.

In 2 batches, transfer vegetables and any remaining liquid to food processor or blender and purée. Return to pan and add all remaining ingredients except orange pieces and sour cream. Simmer, uncovered, over low heat to blend flavors, about 10 minutes longer.

To serve, ladle into individual bowls. Top each serving with a few orange pieces and a spoonful of sour cream. Serve immediately.

Country Vegetable Soup

Similar to a minestrone, this hearty cold-weather soup is made mostly from ingredients found in the pantry. It is a meal in itself. Serve with warm peasant bread.

2 cans (14 ½ ounces each) chicken or beef broth, or a combination

1 cup chopped yellow onion

2 cloves garlic, minced

2 celery stalks, sliced

2 carrots, sliced

2 small new potatoes, peeled and cut into ½-inch dice

1 teaspoon salt

1 can (28 ounces) whole tomatoes, including liquid, tomatoes chopped

1 can (15 ounces) white beans, rinsed and drained

1 zucchini, unpeeled, sliced and slices quartered

½ cup broken vermicelli

¼ cup chopped fresh basil, or 1 teaspoon dried basil, crumbled

Salt and freshly ground pepper to taste

Basil Pesto (page 193), or freshly grated Parmesan cheese, for topping (optional)

Into a large soup pot over high heat, place chicken broth, onion, garlic, celery, carrots, potatoes, and salt. Bring to a boil, reduce heat to medium low and cook, covered, 15 minutes. Add tomatoes, beans, zucchini, vermicelli, and basil.

Bring to a boil again, reduce heat and cook, covered, until zucchini is tender and vermicelli is al dente, about 15 minutes. Season with salt and pepper to taste. Keep warm until serving time. For a thicker soup, transfer 1 cup of soup solids to food processor or blender and blend, then stir back into soup.

Ladle into bowls and serve immediately. Top with a dollop of pesto or Parmesan cheese.

Dilled Zucchini Soup

Dill imparts an extra sparkle to this usually bland soup. Serve with a green salad and crusty bread.

2 large zucchini (about
    1 1/2 pounds), unpeeled
    and sliced
1/2 cup chopped yellow
    onion
1 potato, peeled, halved
    lengthwise, then sliced
1 1/2 cups chicken broth
1 cup buttermilk or milk
1/2 teaspoon salt
1/8 teaspoon pepper
1/2 teaspoon dried dill,
    crumbled
Few drops Tabasco sauce

In a saucepan combine zucchini, onion, potato, and 1 cup broth. Bring to a boil, reduce heat to medium low and cook, covered, until vegetables are tender, about 20 minutes.

Transfer to food processor or blender and purée. Return to pan and add remaining broth, buttermilk, and seasonings. Simmer on low heat to blend flavors, about 10 minutes. Ladle into bowls and serve immediately.

Real Chicken Noodle Soup

Just what the doctor ordered when you are down with a cold and not feeling well. The steaming soup breaks up congestion and soothes dry, sore throats, but it's good even when you're not sick.

1 chicken (2½ pounds), quartered

10 cups water

1 tablespoon black peppercorns

2 celery stalks, sliced

1 carrot, cut into 1-inch pieces

1 onion, quartered

2 cloves garlic, halved

2 fresh basil leaves, or ½ teaspoon dried basil, crumbled

3 sprigs parsley

1 bay leaf

2 teaspoons salt

1 cup wide egg noodles, uncooked

Salt and freshly ground pepper to taste

In a large soup pot over high heat, combine all ingredients except noodles and the additional salt and pepper. Bring to a boil and skim off foam. Reduce heat to medium-low and simmer, covered, until chicken is falling from the bones, about 1 hour. Remove chicken and carrots to a plate to cool. Strain broth into a bowl, and discard solids.

Remove skinned chicken from bones, cut into bite-sized pieces, and set aside. Discard skin and bones. Chop carrots and set aside with chicken. Using a fat separator, remove fat from broth and discard. (If time allows, cool broth in the refrigerator all day or overnight and then remove the layer of fat that forms on the top.)

Return broth to pot and bring to a boil. Add noodles and cook, uncovered, until noodles are al dente, about 10 minutes. Return chicken and carrots to pot, and simmer until heated through, about 10 minutes longer. Season with salt and pepper. Ladle into bowls and serve.

Tomato, Corn, and Sausage Soup

MAKES ABOUT 4 CUPS

Full of flavor and color, this thick soup is just right for a cold winter day. The crushed tortilla chips on top add flavor and texture.

½ pound bulk pork sausage

½ cup chopped yellow onion

½ cup chopped green bell pepper

1 celery stalk, sliced

2 cloves garlic, minced

1 can (14½ ounces) whole tomatoes including juice, tomatoes chopped

2½ cups chicken broth

1 cup fresh or frozen whole corn

¾ teaspoon salt

Freshly ground pepper to taste

Crushed tortilla chips, for garnish

In a large soup pot over medium heat, brown sausage about 5 minutes, breaking up with a spoon as it cooks. Add onion, bell pepper, celery, and garlic, and sauté vegetables until soft, about 5 minutes. Add tomatoes, broth, corn, salt, and pepper.

Simmer on low heat, covered, until flavors are blended, about 20 minutes. Simmer, uncovered, 10 minutes longer or until ready to serve. Serve in bowls and top with crushed tortilla chips, if desired.

Navy Bean Soup

An old-time favorite that is still popular with all ages. Make this when you have a leftover pork or ham bone to cook along with the beans for extra flavor. Serve with crusty French bread and a wedge of lettuce with your favorite dressing.

2 cups navy beans, sorted and rinsed
10 cups water
1 pork or ham bone
1 bay leaf
1 yellow onion, chopped
3 celery stalks, sliced
1 or 2 cloves garlic, minced
1 teaspoon salt
Freshly ground pepper to taste

Place beans in a large soup pot with water. Bring to a boil and boil 2 minutes. Remove from heat, cover, and let stand 1 hour. Add meat bone and bay leaf. Cover and simmer 1 hour, then add onion, celery, and garlic and cook over medium-low heat, uncovered, until beans and vegetables are tender, stirring several times, about 1 hour longer.

Remove bone and cut off any meat from bone and return to soup. Remove bay leaf and discard. Mash some of the beans with the back of a spoon against the side of the pan until soup is of desired consistency. Soup will thicken as it cooks. Season with salt and pepper. Keep hot until ready to serve.

Spicy Black Bean Soup

For a quick warm-up on a cold winter day, serve this full-bodied black bean soup with assorted toppings. Serve with Orange, Cucumber, and Jícama Salad with Lime-Cumin Dressing (page 74), and Cheese Bread (page 149).

2 cups black beans, sorted
   and rinsed
7 cups water
1 tablespoon vegetable oil
1 large yellow onion,
   chopped
1 green bell pepper, seeded
   and chopped
1 carrot, chopped
2 celery stalks, sliced
2 cloves garlic, minced
4 cups water
4 cups chicken broth
3/4 teaspoon ground cumin
1/4 teaspoon cayenne
1/4 teaspoon ground
   coriander
1/2 teaspoon dried oregano
1/2 teaspoon chili powder
1 bay leaf
1 teaspoon salt
Freshly ground pepper
   to taste
1/4 cup sherry or dry white
   wine (optional)

GARNISHES
Grated Monterey Jack cheese
Sour cream or plain yogurt
2 hard-cooked eggs, chopped
Green onions, sliced
Lime wedges

In a large soup pot over high heat place beans and water. Boil, uncovered, 2 minutes; remove from heat. Cover and let stand 1 hour.

In a skillet warm oil over medium heat. Add vegetables and sauté until tender, about 10 minutes.

Drain beans, return to soup pot, and add 4 cups water, 4 cups chicken broth, sautéed vegetables, and seasonings except salt and pepper. Bring to a boil, reduce heat to medium-low or low and simmer, covered, until beans are tender, about 2 1/4 hours, stirring occasionally.

Remove bay leaf and discard. Season with salt and pepper. Transfer soup to food processor or blender and purée in batches to desired consistency. Return soup to pan and reheat. Season with sherry if using. Ladle into bowls and pass the garnishes.

Friday Clam Chowder

This can be made with bacon or without; it is good either way. It is a medium-thick soup with lots of potatoes and clams. More milk may be added according to taste.

5 to 6 cups raw peeled and cubed potatoes

1 celery stalk, sliced

2 carrots, chopped

1 cup chopped yellow onion

1 cup water

2 cans (6 1/2 ounces each) chopped clams (drain juice and reserve)

1 tablespoon all-purpose flour

2 1/2 to 3 cups whole milk

1 teaspoon salt

Freshly ground pepper to taste

4 slices bacon, cooked and crumbled (optional)

Butter, for topping (optional)

Paprika, for topping

In a saucepan over medium heat place potatoes, celery, carrots, onion, water, and reserved clam juice. Bring to a boil. Reduce heat to low and simmer, covered, until vegetables are very soft, about 15 minutes. Sprinkle with flour and stir until blended. Add drained clams, milk, salt, pepper, and bacon, if using. Simmer, uncovered, 5 to 10 minutes.

Ladle into bowls, add a pat of butter, and sprinkle with paprika. Serve immediately.

Northwest Seafood Chowder

Traditionally in many families, seafood chowder is served on the eve of a big holiday dinner. This chowder is a tasty combination of seafood, vegetables, and seasonings. Seafood can vary according to tastes and availability.

2 to 3 tablespoons butter or margarine

½ cup chopped yellow onion

¾ cup chopped celery

1 carrot, grated

3 cups cubed potatoes

2 cups chicken broth

1 teaspoon salt

¼ teaspoon dried thyme, crumbled

¼ teaspoon freshly ground pepper

1 bay leaf

¼ cup flour

½ cup cold water

1 cup whole milk

1 can (6½ ounces) chopped clams including juice

½ pound white fish, cut into bite-sized pieces

½ pound small scallops

¼ pound cooked, small shrimp

⅓ pound small oysters, halved (optional; see note)

¼ cup chopped parsley

In a large soup pot over medium heat melt butter. Add onion, celery, and carrot and sauté until vegetables are slightly tender, 8 to 10 minutes.

Add potatoes, broth, and seasonings and bring to a boil over high heat; then reduce temperature to medium-low or low and cook, covered, until vegetables are tender, about 15 minutes. Remove bay leaf and discard.

In a small bowl or cup blend flour and water. Stir flour mixture into soup and stir until thickened, about 1 minute. Add milk and clams and mix well.

Add seafood and simmer, covered, until flavors are blended, about 10 minutes longer. Ladle into bowls and sprinkle with parsley. Serve immediately.

Note: If oysters are omitted, increase white fish to ¾ pound.

Thick Spaghetti Soup

A perfect soup to serve friends or family while they are watching a football game on TV or for a Sunday night supper. Serve with garlic bread and vegetable strips.

1/2 pound ground beef

1/2 pound bulk sausage

1 cup chopped yellow onion

2 cloves garlic, minced

1 can (28 ounces) Italian-style tomatoes with basil, including juices (break up tomatoes; see note)

2 cups beef broth

1 cup tomato juice

1 teaspoon salt

1/4 teaspoon dried oregano, crumbled

1/4 teaspoon dried basil, crumbled

1 bay leaf

Freshly ground pepper to taste

1/4 cup chopped parsley

1 cup broken (1-inch lengths) spaghetti

1 cup fresh or frozen peas, thawed

1/2 cup sliced black olives

Freshly grated Parmesan or Asagio cheese, for topping

In a large saucepan or soup pot over medium-high heat, cook beef, sausage, onion, and garlic, stirring and breaking up meats into small pieces. Cook until meats are no longer pink and vegetables are soft, about 10 minutes, stirring occasionally.

Pour off any excess grease from pan. Add tomatoes and juices, broth, tomato juice, seasonings, parsley, and spaghetti. Cover and simmer over low heat until flavors are blended, about 30 minutes. Add peas and olives and cook, uncovered, 10 minutes longer or until ready to serve. Remove bay leaf and discard.

Ladle into individual bowls, sprinkle with cheese, and serve immediately.

Note: To break up tomatoes, use a pair of stainless-steel kitchen scissors, and cut up tomatoes while they are still in the can.

Chilled Avocado Soup

Serve this refreshing soup on a warm day as a first course or as the main course for a summer luncheon.

2 ripe avocados, halved
  and pitted
1 can (14 1/2 ounces)
  chicken broth
1/2 cup light sour cream,
  or plain nonfat yogurt
1/4 teaspoon salt
3 drops Tabasco sauce
Paprika, for sprinkling
  on top

Scoop out avocado pulp and place in food processor along with broth, sour cream, salt, and Tabasco sauce. Process until smooth. Transfer to another container, cover, and chill several hours. Ladle into chilled bowls. Sprinkle with paprika.

The Salad Bowl

Tossed green salads may be served
as an introductory course, with
the entrée, or after the main
course, European style. With the
introduction of unusual greens,
nut oils, and fruit vinegars, green
salads have taken on a new
dimension. With the prewashed
packages of mixed greens that can
be found in most produce
departments, the time-consuming
tasks of washing
and drying are
eliminated.
The addition of nuts,
fruits, fresh herbs,
cheeses, olives, and
croutons give color, texture,
and interest to a salad.

Vegetable Salad Basics

- Select crisp, fresh greens and vegetables that are firm and free from blemishes.

- Use a variety of greens for contrasting flavors, texture, and color.

- Store most salad ingredients in plastic bags in the refrigerator. Mushrooms should be stored in a paper bag. Tomatoes should be stored at room temperature but used within a day or two. To ripen tomatoes, put them in a closed paper bag.

- Wash greens and vegetables before using and dry thoroughly. A salad spinner works well for drying greens.

- Tear greens into bite-sized pieces unless otherwise stated in recipe.

- Allow 1 cup lightly packed greens per serving plus 1 or 2 cups extra.

- Salad greens and vegetables may be combined in a bowl several hours in advance, covered, and refrigerated, but do not add dressing until serving time.

- Toss salad lightly with dressing just before serving to prevent wilting. Use only enough dressing to coat the ingredients. Overdressing can ruin a good salad.

- Use homemade dressings for best results. They are more healthful and flavorful and easy to make.

Fruit Salad Basics

Fruit salads are cool and refreshing and are often served with a hearty meal. They are especially popular in the summer when seasonal fruit is available. Many exotic and tropical fruits are now also available in the markets and add variety to a salad. With fruit salads you can be creative, so make your own combinations with contrasting colors, shapes, and flavors. Fruit salads are also served as a light dessert with dressing on the side.

Arrange fruits in a pretty glass bowl, compote, or on a decorative tray and garnish with mint leaves or flowers.

Select summer fruits that are slightly soft to the touch when pressed and are free of blemishes and bruises. Ripe fruits will have a delightful fragrance. Fruits shipped in out of season, such as apricots, pears, peaches, and plums, are generally picked before fully ripe. To ripen after purchase, place in a paper bag and loosely close.

Wash, dry, and store, uncovered, in the refrigerator.

Allow ¾ to 1 cup fruit per serving.

Prepare salads just before serving. To prevent apples from discoloring, dip cut slices in water with lemon juice.

Drain well before serving.

Add dressing, if desired, or serve it in a separate bowl.

Pasta and Grain Salad Basics

Pasta and grain salads can be served as a main course or as an accompaniment to the entrée to add variety to the meal. They are great to take to picnics, potlucks, or tailgate parties (always transport in a cooler chest).

Rinse cooked pasta under cold water and cool slightly.

Combine with other ingredients 4 to 5 hours before serving and chill thoroughly.

Oil-based dressings can be added in advance but creamy dressings should be added no more than 1 to 2 hours before serving. (If dressing is added too soon, the dressing is absorbed into the pasta and more dressing is required, adding extra calories.)

Spinach, Pear, and Walnut Salad with Raspberry Vinaigrette

SERVES 6 TO 8

Make this tossed salad with a sweet-tart dressing in winter when fresh pears are in season.

1 package (6 ounces, about 8 cups) prewashed spinach, stems removed, and torn into bite-sized pieces

¼ cup toasted walnuts (page 55), coarsely chopped

2 ripe pears, peeled, cored, and cut into bite-sized pieces

¼ cup chopped red onion

½ cup crumbled blue cheese

Raspberry Vinaigrette (recipe follows)

In a large salad bowl mix all ingredients together and toss with vinaigrette.

Raspberry Vinaigrette

¼ cup raspberry vinegar

¼ cup olive oil

¼ cup vegetable oil

2 cloves garlic, minced

¼ teaspoon sugar

¼ teaspoon salt

Freshly ground pepper to taste

In a small bowl whisk together all ingredients until well mixed. Transfer to a jar with tight-fitting lid and refrigerate until well chilled. Shake well before using.

Makes about ¾ cup

Greek Salad with Feta Cheese

A Greek salad usually does not include lettuce because greens are not plentiful in Greece. However, this version has the authentic flavor.

1 head red-leaf lettuce, torn into bite-sized pieces, about 8 cups

1 cucumber, peeled, halved, seeded, and sliced

1/2 red or green bell pepper, seeded and cut into large bite-sized pieces

1/2 red onion, sliced and separated into rings

1/2 cup pitted Kalamata olives, or ripe olives

1/2 cup crumbled feta cheese

2 tomatoes, seeded, cut into wedges, and halved

Lemony Dressing (page 70)

In a large salad bowl combine all ingredients and toss with dressing to moisten.

49

Caesar Salad, San Francisco Style

SERVES 4

This Caesar salad calls for whole or sliced romaine leaves and is not tossed. Garlic bread crumbs are sprinkled on top instead of croutons.

1 head romaine lettuce (use smaller, tender, inner leaves only; reserve outer leaves for another salad)

Garlic Crumbs (recipe follows)

Creamy Caesar Dressing (recipe follows)

Shaved Parmesan cheese, for topping

Arrange 3 or 4 whole or sliced romaine leaves on 4 chilled individual plates (oval plates if available). Add 1 to 2 tablespoons of dressing in a strip down the center of the greens. Add about 3 tablespoons of garlic crumbs to each salad. Top with several shavings (use potato peeler) of Parmesan cheese. Serve very cold.

Garlic Crumbs

4 or 5 slices sourdough bread (depending on size) to make about 2 cups coarse crumbs

2 tablespoons butter

1 tablespoon vegetable oil

1 large clove garlic, minced

Tear up bread into large chunks and let air dry for several hours.

Preheat oven to 325°F. Place bread in food processor and process slightly. Crumbs should be very coarse. In a small nonstick frying pan, melt butter with oil and garlic over medium-high heat and sauté briefly. Add crumbs and toss to coat. Stir constantly until crumbs are golden and crisp, 3 to 4 minutes.

Creamy Caesar Dressing

This dressing has just a hint of anchovy. The amount of anchovies may vary depending on your taste.

1 to 2 teaspoons anchovy paste, or 1 or 2 anchovy fillets, drained

1 large clove garlic, cut up

2 tablespoons freshly ground Parmesan cheese

½ cup light mayonnaise

¼ cup plain nonfat yogurt

1 tablespoon red wine vinegar

1 tablespoon fresh lemon juice

½ teaspoon Worcestershire sauce

1 tablespoon vegetable oil

Freshly ground pepper to taste

In food processor or blender place all ingredients and process until smooth. Cover and refrigerate until ready to use.

Makes about 1¼ cups

Garden Salad with Variations

Variations on this salad may be made according to the taste and availability of ingredients. Make your own combinations and select a complementary dressing.

6 cups assorted salad greens

1 red onion, sliced and separated into rings

2 avocados, sliced

2 tomatoes, cut in wedges

1 cucumber, halved lengthwise and seeded, then sliced

Italian Dressing (page 56), Homemade Ranch Dressing (recipe follows), or Sevé French Dressing (recipe follows)

In a large salad bowl toss greens and vegetables with dressing to coat. Serve immediately.

Variations:

• Substitute 6 green onions including some tender green tops, sliced, for red onion.

• Top with grated carrots.

• Add jícama strips.

• Add ¼ cup halved ripe olives.

• Add toasted sunflower seeds.

• Add garlic croutons.

Homemade Ranch Dressing

This dressing is far superior to the purchased mix and just as easy to make.

1 cup light mayonnaise
½ cup buttermilk
1 clove garlic, minced
1 green onion including
    some tender green tops,
    cut up
4 parsley sprigs
¼ teaspoon celery salt
¼ teaspoon seasoned salt

Place all ingredients in food processor or blender and process until smooth. Cover and refrigerate until ready to use.

Makes about 1½ cups

Jevé French Dressing

A just right balance of contrasting flavors makes this sweet-and-sour dressing good on any green salad.

⅔ cup catsup
⅔ cup vegetable oil
¼ cup honey
¼ cup cider vinegar
¼ teaspoon Worcestershire
    sauce
1 teaspoon fresh lemon
    juice
¼ teaspoon salt

Combine all ingredients in a jar with tight-fitting lid, shake well, and refrigerate. Shake well again before using.

Makes about 2 cups

California Salad with Tarragon–Sesame Seed Dressing

SERVES 6

Juicy, sweet oranges, buttery avocado, red onion, and leaf lettuce in a sweet tarragon dressing make a salad that goes well with seafood.

1 head leaf lettuce, torn into bite-sized pieces

2 oranges, peeled, cut into bite-sized pieces, and drained

1 avocado, peeled, pitted, and sliced

1/2 red onion, sliced and rings separated

Tarragon-Sesame Seed Dressing (recipe follows)

In a large bowl combine lettuce, oranges, avocado, and onion. Toss with just enough dressing to moisten and serve immediately.

Tarragon–Sesame Seed Dressing

1/2 cup vegetable oil

3 tablespoons white wine vinegar

1/2 teaspoon dried tarragon

2 teaspoons sugar

1/4 teaspoon salt

1/2 teaspoon dry mustard

1/4 teaspoon paprika

1 tablespoon toasted sesame seeds (see note)

In a jar with a lid combine all ingredients and whisk until blended. Shake well before using. Store in refrigerator.

Makes about 1/2 cup

Note: To toast sesame seeds, place them in a small nonstick skillet and stir on medium-high heat until golden, about 2 minutes.

Mesclun Salad with Feta Cheese and Walnuts and Balsamic Vinaigrette

SERVES 6

Mesclun (also known as baby greens or field greens) adds elegance to a salad. It is a combination of a variety of greens of contrasting textures and flavors, and can be purchased, prewashed, in most produce departments.

6 to 8 cups mesclun or other mixed greens
1/2 cup crumbled feta cheese
1/2 cup toasted walnuts, coarsely chopped (see note)
1 red onion, thinly sliced and rings separated
Balsamic Vinaigrette (recipe follows)

In a large salad bowl combine greens with cheese, walnuts, and onion and toss with enough dressing to coat. Serve immediately.

Note: To toast walnuts, preheat oven to 350°F, place nuts on a baking sheet and place in oven. Toast, stirring once or twice, for 5 minutes. Cool before using.

Balsamic Vinaigrette

2/3 cup olive oil
3 tablespoons balsamic vinegar (see note)
2 teaspoons fresh lemon juice
1 clove garlic, minced
1 tablespoon chopped fresh basil, or 1/4 teaspoon dried basil
1/2 teaspoon sugar
1/2 teaspoon salt
1/8 teaspoon pepper

Combine all ingredients in a jar with tight-fitting lid. Shake well before using.

Makes about 1 cup

Note: Balsamic vinegar is a sweet aromatic vinegar produced in Italy. If this is unavailable, you can substitute red wine vinegar.

Romaine–Bacon–Apple Salad

The apple slices add texture and color to the salad.

1 head romaine lettuce, torn into bite-sized pieces

6 slices lean bacon, cooked and crumbled

1/3 cup freshly grated Parmesan cheese

1 red apple, unpeeled and sliced

Italian Dressing (recipe follows)

In a large salad bowl, mix all ingredients together. Refrigerate until chilled. Toss with dressing to moisten just before serving.

Italian Dressing

1/4 cup olive oil

1/4 cup vegetable oil

1 clove garlic, minced

2 tablespoons red wine vinegar

1 tablespoon fresh lemon juice

1/4 teaspoon salt

1/4 teaspoon dried oregano, crumbled

1/4 teaspoon dried thyme, crumbled

1/4 teaspoon dried basil, crumbled

Freshly ground pepper to taste

In a small bowl whisk all ingredients together. Cover and refrigerate until ready to use.

Makes about ½ cup

Spinach Salad with Mushrooms, Blue Cheese, and Bacon

SERVES 6 TO 8

The addition of mushrooms, blue cheese, and bacon makes this spinach salad special. For convenience, buy the prewashed spinach in a bag, found in most supermarkets.

6 to 8 cups fresh spinach, washed, stems removed and torn into bite-sized pieces

8 fresh mushrooms, sliced

1/2 red onion, sliced and separated into rings

8 to 10 lean bacon slices, cooked and crumbled

1/2 cup crumbled blue cheese

Dijon Dressing (page 63)

Combine all ingredients in a large bowl and toss with dressing to moisten.

Variation: Omit bacon and add one or both of the following: 1/3 cup coarsely chopped walnuts; 1/3 cup chopped red bell pepper.

Thick Tomato Slices with Avocado Dressing and Toasted Hazelnuts

An easy summer salad to serve at a barbecue or picnic. Add dressing and nuts just before serving.

Lettuce leaves, for
   lining platter
4 to 6 large tomatoes,
   cut into thick slices
Avocado Dressing
   (recipe follows)
1/3 cup chopped toasted
   hazelnuts (see note)
Watercress sprigs, for
   garnish

Line a platter with lettuce leaves. Arrange tomatoes on lettuce leaves. Spread some of the dressing on top of tomatoes, but do not cover completely. Sprinkle with hazelnuts. Garnish with watercress. Pass remaining dressing in a bowl. Serve immediately.

Variation: Add avocado slices.

Note: To toast hazelnuts, preheat oven to 350°F. Spread nuts on a baking sheet and bake until lightly colored and skins are blistered, 12 to 15 minutes. Wrap hot nuts in clean towel to steam 1 minute. Then rub the nuts in the towel to remove most of the skins.

Avocado Dressing

1 ripe avocado, peeled, pitted, and cut up

½ cup plain nonfat yogurt

½ cup light mayonnaise

1 tablespoon white wine vinegar

1 tablespoons fresh lemon juice

1 clove garlic, cut up

1 green onion, including some tender green tops, cut up

2 fresh parsley sprigs, cut up

1 teaspoon Worcestershire sauce

¼ teaspoon Beau Monde seasoning

¼ teaspoon salt

¼ teaspoon dry mustard

Freshly ground pepper to taste

In food processor or blender, combine all ingredients. Process until smooth. Cover and refrigerate.

Makes about 1½ cups

Avocado Mexican Salad

Avocados topped with a relish-type filling go well with grilled meats or Mexican food. Serve with warm tortillas.

2 tomatoes, seeded, diced, and drained

1 cucumber, seeded and diced

1/4 cup chopped green bell pepper

1/2 cup chopped red onion

3/4 cup garbanzo beans, rinsed and drained

2 tablespoons chopped fresh parsley or cilantro

Lime-Cumin Dressing (recipe follows)

3 ripe avocados

2 tablespoons lemon juice

Lettuce leaves

In a large bowl combine vegetables, beans, and parsley or cilantro. Add dressing and mix well. Cover and marinate for several hours in refrigerator.

Just before serving, peel avocados, cut in half and remove pits. Brush with lemon juice. Place lettuce leaves on a platter or on individual plates and add avocados. Using a slotted spoon, fill each avocado half with marinated mixture. Serve immediately.

Lime-Cumin Dressing

Juice of 1 lime

1 tablespoon white wine vinegar

3 tablespoons vegetable oil

3 tablespoons olive oil

1 tablespoon honey

1/4 teaspoon dried oregano, crumbled

1/4 teaspoon ground cumin

1/4 teaspoon dry mustard

1/4 teaspoon salt

1/4 teaspoon white pepper

In a small bowl whisk all ingredients well.

Makes 3/4 cup

Cashew Coleslaw

The nuts and curry give this coleslaw a Middle Eastern accent. This is a salad that goes well with lamb.

6 cups shredded cabbage

¼ cup chopped unsalted cashews or peanuts

3 green onions including some tender green tops, sliced

Slaw Dressing (recipe follows)

Place all ingredients in a bowl. Mix with dressing and chill several hours before serving.

Slaw Dressing

⅓ cup light mayonnaise

¼ cup light sour cream

1 teaspoon prepared mustard

¼ teaspoon curry powder

¼ teaspoon salt

1 teaspoon white wine vinegar

Freshly ground pepper to taste

In a small bowl mix all ingredients together until smooth.

Makes about ⅔ cup

New Potato and Green Bean Salad

A perfect summer salad to serve for a barbecue or picnic. It should be made ahead to allow flavors to mellow.

½ teaspoon salt, for water

6 to 7 medium red-skinned potatoes (about 2 pounds), unpeeled

½ pound fresh green beans, trimmed

½ cup chopped red onion

4 or 5 fresh basil leaves, slivered

3 tablespoons chopped parsley

Dijon Dressing (recipe follows)

Salt and pepper to taste

In a large saucepan bring enough salted water to cover potatoes to a boil. Add potatoes, reduce heat to medium-low and gently boil until tender, about 20 minutes. Drain and rinse with cold water to stop the cooking process; drain again. Set aside to cool. When cool, cut potatoes into bite-sized pieces and place in a large bowl.

Place beans in same large saucepan with water to cover. Bring to a boil, reduce heat to medium, and cook beans until tender crisp, about 5 minutes. Drain under cold water to stop the cooking process. Pat dry, cut in half, and add to bowl holding potatoes. Add onion, basil, and parsley.

Toss with Dijon Dressing and season with salt and pepper. Cover and refrigerate at least 6 hours. Serve cold or at room temperature.

Dijon Dressing

1/4 cup red wine vinegar

2 teaspoons Dijon mustard

1 tablespoon fresh lemon juice

1 clove garlic, minced

1/4 teaspoon Worcestershire sauce

2 drops Tabasco sauce

1/2 teaspoon sugar

1/4 teaspoon salt

Freshly ground pepper to taste

1/2 cup olive oil

In a bowl combine all ingredients except oil. Slowly whisk in oil. Cover and refrigerate until ready to use.

Makes about 3/4 cup

Cucumber and Red Onion Salad with Dill Dressing

Cucumbers are available year-round, but fresh, vine-ripened cucumbers are the best. Serve with grilled salmon or halibut.

2 large cucumbers, peeled
1/2 red onion, sliced and separated into rings
1 small red bell pepper, seeded and chopped
Dill Dressing (recipe follows)

Halve cucumbers lengthwise and scrape seeds out with a spoon. Slice horizontally into 1/4-inch slices.

In a bowl combine cucumber slices, onion rings, and bell pepper, and mix with dressing. Cover and chill several hours or overnight.

Dill Dressing

1/2 cup light sour cream
1/4 cup plain nonfat yogurt
1 tablespoon white wine vinegar
1 tablespoon fresh lemon juice
1 teaspoon sugar
1 tablespoon fresh dill, or 1 teaspoon dill weed
1/2 teaspoon salt
Freshly ground pepper to taste

In a bowl whisk all ingredients together.

Makes about 1 cup

64

Fresh Pea and Snap Pea Salad

A summertime salad of fresh shelled peas, snap peas, jícama, and bacon with a creamy dressing.

1 cup snap peas (about ¼ pound), trimmed and halved crosswise

2 cups fresh shelled small peas or 1 package (10 ounces) frozen peas, thawed and rinsed in hot water

¼ cup diced red onion

¾ cup diced jícama or celery

6 slices bacon, cooked until crisp and crumbled

Creamy Mayonnaise Dressing (recipe follows)

In a bowl combine peas, onion, jícama, and bacon. Add enough dressing to coat and mix well. Cover and refrigerate several hours.

Creamy Mayonnaise Dressing

¼ cup mayonnaise

¼ cup sour cream or plain nonfat yogurt

1 teaspoon fresh lemon juice

1 teaspoon sugar

¼ teaspoon salt

¼ teaspoon dried basil, crumbled

Freshly ground pepper to taste

In a small bowl stir together all ingredients until smooth.

Makes about ½ cup

Vegetables Marinated with Fresh Herbs

Carrots and beans are cooked al dente and then marinated overnight in a zesty dressing; other vegetables are added later. This is a good salad to take to a tailgate party or picnic.

3 carrots, sliced diagonally into ½-inch slices

½ pound fresh green beans, trimmed

Reed's Own Dressing (page 73)

8 to 10 mushrooms, sliced

½ red onion, sliced and separated into rings

1 cup cherry tomatoes, halved

1 cup pitted ripe olives

2 tablespoons chopped fresh basil

1 tablespoon chopped fresh rosemary

¼ cup chopped parsley

Place carrots in a steamer rack over gently boiling water, cover, and steam 5 minutes. Add beans to the carrots and steam until vegetables are tender crisp, about 6 minutes longer. Drain and rinse under cold water to stop cooking process.

Place carrots and beans in a bowl; add dressing to coat vegetables and mix well. Cover and marinate 6 hours or overnight in the refrigerate. Two hours before serving, stir in remaining ingredients. Re-cover and refrigerate until serving time.

Spinach and Shrimp Salad

SERVES 6

This salad goes well with any meat entrée. Medium shrimp or small salad shrimp that are sold already cooked may be substituted.

½ pound medium shrimp, peeled and deveined

6 to 8 cups torn spinach leaves

¼ pound bean sprouts, rinsed, drained, and dried

½ white onion, sliced and rings separated

Sevé French Dressing (page 53)

In a saucepan cover shrimp with water. Boil over medium-high heat until shrimp turn pink, 1 to 2 minutes. Drain and cool. In a large bowl mix with remaining ingredients and toss with dressing.

Composed Salad with Shrimp, Mushrooms, and Sprouts

This salad has an Oriental flair that complements pork. Cook and marinate the shrimp several hours before serving.

¼ teaspoon salt, for water

12 medium shrimp, cleaned and deveined

Oriental Dressing (recipe follows)

6 large mushrooms, sliced

6 cups washed spinach, stems removed, and leaves torn into bite-sized pieces

1 cup bean sprouts, rinsed and dried

6 green onions including some tender green tops, sliced

In a saucepan over medium-high heat bring to a boil enough salted water to cover shrimp. Cook shrimp, uncovered, until they turn pink, 1 to 2 minutes. Drain and cool slightly; then marinate in 2 tablespoons of the dressing for several hours, covered, in the refrigerator. Mix mushrooms with 2 tablespoons of the dressing just before serving.

To assemble, place 1 cup spinach on each of 6 individual salad plates. Arrange mushrooms, bean sprouts, and shrimp on top, dividing evenly. Sprinkle with onions and drizzle with dressing.

Oriental Dressing

¼ cup white wine vinegar

1 teaspoon soy sauce

½ teaspoon Worcestershire sauce

1 large clove garlic, minced

1 teaspoon sugar

½ teaspoon dry mustard

¼ to ½ teaspoon curry powder

½ teaspoon salt

Freshly ground pepper to taste

⅔ cup vegetable oil

In a jar or bowl mix all ingredients, except oil. Whisk in oil slowly. Cover and refrigerate until ready to use. Mix well before using.

Makes about 1 cup

Greek Pasta Salad

This Greek-inspired salad goes well with grilled meats, especially lamb. It also makes a nice luncheon or picnic salad. Make several hours ahead and chill well.

8 ounces rigatoni, cooked, rinsed, drained, and cooled

1 red bell pepper, seeded and cut into bite-sized pieces

1 cucumber, peeled, seeded, and sliced

1/2 cup chopped red onion

4 ounces feta cheese, crumbled

1/2 to 3/4 cup Kalamata olives, pits removed, or ripe olives

1/4 cup chopped parsley (optional)

Lemony Dressing (recipe follows)

Tomato wedges, for garnish

In a large bowl stir together all ingredients. Cover and refrigerate at least 3 hours. Mix again before serving. Garnish with tomato wedges.

Lemony Dressing

Juice of 1 lemon

2 or 3 cloves garlic, minced

1 teaspoon Dijon mustard

1/4 teaspoon dried thyme, crumbled

1/2 teaspoon dried oregano, crumbled

1/2 teaspoon sugar

1/4 teaspoon salt

Freshly ground pepper to taste

1/3 cup olive oil

In a small bowl stir together all ingredients except olive oil. Whisk in olive oil slowly. Cover and chill until ready to use.

Makes 2/3 cup

Couscous Salad

This refreshing salad is similar to tabbouleh but made with couscous instead of the traditional bulgur. It makes a wonderful picnic salad or main luncheon salad. Serve Pocket Bread Wedges (page 25) on the side.

1 1/4 cups couscous

2 cups boiling chicken broth or water

1 cup chopped fresh parsley

1/2 cup chopped green onion including some tender green tops

1/4 cup chopped fresh mint leaves

2 cloves garlic, minced

3 to 4 plum tomatoes, chopped (about 2 cups)

1 small cucumber, seeded and diced

Lemony Dressing (page 70)

Mint leaves for garnish

Place couscous in a large bowl and add boiling broth.

Cover and let stand 5 minutes. Fluff with a fork and cool slightly. Add parsley, onion, mint, garlic, tomatoes, and cucumber. Add dressing to coat and stir gently to mix well.

Cover and refrigerate several hours before using. Garnish with mint leaves.

Tortellini Salad

Tortellini can be found in the refrigerator section of most supermarkets. Combined with vegetables, they make a hearty summer salad for picnics and barbecues. Make several hours in advance to blend flavors.

2 1/2 quarts water

1 package (9 ounces) cheese tortellini

1/2 red bell pepper, seeded, cut into 1/2-inch strips and then thirds

5 or 6 mushrooms, sliced

1/2 cup chopped celery

1/2 cup chopped red onion

1 cup canned artichoke hearts, halved and drained (optional)

1/4 cup chopped parsley

1/4 cup chopped fresh basil leaves

1/2 cup sliced ripe olives

Salt and freshly ground pepper to taste

Reed's Own Dressing (recipe follows)

2 tomatoes, cut into wedges, for garnish

In a large pot of gently boiling water, cook tortellini until al dente, about 7 minutes. Drain well and transfer to a bowl. Combine with remaining ingredients. Toss with just enough dressing to coat (about 1/3 cup). Cover and refrigerate several hours or overnight. Add more dressing just before serving, if needed. Garnish with tomatoes.

Reed's Own Dressing

A zesty dressing good on all salads, especially pasta salads.

1/2 cup vegetable oil

1/4 cup olive oil

1/3 cup red wine vinegar

2 cloves garlic, cut up

1 green onion including
   some tender green tops,
   cut up

2 fresh parsley sprigs,
   cut up

1/4 teaspoon salt

1/4 teaspoon dried thyme

1/4 teaspoon dried oregano

1/4 teaspoon dried basil

1/4 teaspoon celery salt

1/4 teaspoon pepper

1/4 teaspoon paprika

1 tablespoon freshly
   grated Parmesan cheese

1 teaspoon Dijon mustard

In food processor or blender combine all ingredients. Process until well blended. Transfer to a jar with tight-fitting lid and refrigerate until chilled. Shake well before using.

Makes about 1 cup

Orange, Cucumber, and Jícama Salad

Sliced oranges, cucumber slices, and jícama strips with a sweet-tart dressing make a good salad to serve with Mexican food.

Shredded lettuce

4 oranges, peeled, white membrane removed, and sliced

1 cucumber, peeled and sliced

1 small jícama, peeled and cut into strips like French fries

¼ cup chopped red onion

¼ cup chopped green bell pepper

Lime-Cumin Dressing (page 60)

Parsley or cilantro sprigs, for garnish

Line a platter with lettuce. Arrange oranges, cucumbers, and jícama in groups on lettuce. Sprinkle with onion and pepper. Drizzle about half of the dressing over the salad.

Garnish with parsley or cilantro sprigs, cover, and chill several hours. Pass remaining dressing in a small pitcher or bowl.

Pear Salad with Blue Cheese Topping

In this recipe, delicate juicy pears are complemented by blue cheese. Fresh pears are usually sold green in the market, so they must be fully ripened at home before using. Allow two to three days for ripening. When they are yellow and soft to the touch, they are ready to use.

2 large, ripe, fresh pears, preferably Comice or Bartlett (see note)

1/3 cup light cream cheese, at room temperature

2 tablespoons crumbled blue cheese

2 teaspoons fresh orange juice

Lettuce leaves, for lining plate

1/4 cup chopped walnuts

Peel pears, halve, and remove core. In a small bowl blend cheeses and orange juice. Line 4 salad plates with lettuce leaves. Place 1 pear half on each plate. Divide cheese mixture equally among pears. Sprinkle with walnuts.

Note: If peeling pears ahead, brush with lemon juice to prevent their discoloring.

Summer Fruit Platter with Curry Dressing

On a decorative platter or tray make a colorful array of seasonal fruits of your choice. Serve with Curry Dressing. Allow about 1 cup assorted fruit per serving.

6 to 8 watermelon spears, peeled

6 to 8 cantaloupe spears, peeled

2 bunches green grapes

2 cups raspberries or strawberries

1½ cups blueberries

Mint leaves, for garnish

⅓ cup chopped almonds or walnuts

Curry Dressing (recipe follows)

Arrange fruit in groups on a platter. Tuck in mint leaves. Sprinkle with nuts. Pass the dressing in a separate bowl.

Curry Dressing

½ cup light mayonnaise

½ cup plain nonfat yogurt

1 teaspoon sugar

½ teaspoon curry powder

1 teaspoon soy sauce

In a small bowl mix all ingredients together, cover, and refrigerate until ready to use.

Makes about 1 cup

Assorted Fruit with Honey-Yogurt Sauce

For a no-fuss salad, use this combination of assorted fruits to create a winter fruit platter. Offer the tangy-sweet sauce in a bowl on the side. Other fruits may be used, depending on what is available.

Romaine or kale leaves, for lining platter

2 fresh pears, peeled and sliced

1 red apple, unpeeled, cored, and sliced

1 green apple, unpeeled, cored, and sliced

2 oranges, peeled and sliced

1 bunch green seedless grapes

1 bunch red seedless grapes

Lemon juice, if needed

Honey-Yogurt Sauce (recipe follows)

Line a platter or tray with leaves. Arrange fruit in groups on leaves. If made ahead, brush cut fruit with lemon juice to prevent discoloring. Serve with Honey-Yogurt Sauce.

Honey-Yogurt Sauce

³/₄ cup plain nonfat yogurt

1 tablespoon light mayonnaise

1 tablespoon honey

1 tablespoon poppy seeds

Dash of ground nutmeg

In a small bowl stir together all ingredients. Cover and refrigerate until well chilled.

Makes about 1 cup

Metro Salad

This is a delicious combination of chicken or turkey and apples tossed with Seasoned Mayonnaise. Serve it with cheese bread for a luncheon or light meal.

3 cups cooked chicken or turkey, cut into bite-sized pieces

2 green apples (Granny Smith), unpeeled, cored, and cut into bite-sized pieces

Juice of 1/2 lemon

2 tablespoons chopped parsley

3 tablespoons toasted slivered almonds, for topping, (see note)

Leaf lettuce, for lining plates

Seasoned Mayonnaise (recipe follows)

In a bowl combine all ingredients except almonds and lettuce, and toss with dressing. Cover and refrigerate several hours. Line 4 plates with lettuce leaves. Divide mixture evenly among the plates. Top with almonds.

Note: To toast almonds, preheat oven to 400°F. Spread nuts in a small pan and bake until lightly toasted, about 8 minutes.

Seasoned Mayonnaise

1/2 cup light mayonnaise

1 tablespoon dry white wine

1 teaspoon dried oregano, crumbled

1/4 teaspoon salt

1/8 teaspoon white pepper

In a small bowl combine all ingredients.

Makes about 1/2 cup

Poultry Plus

*Poultry is consumed in almost every part of the world.
Healthful, versatile, and economical, it is used in
a tremendous variety of recipes ranging from elegant
company dinners to family fare.
Generally low in fat, chicken and turkey have become
more popular in recent years because of concerns about
cholesterol and fat in the diet.*

Poultry Basics

- Select chicken and turkey with smooth, tight skin and plump breasts and thighs. Prepackaged poultry should not have liquid in the bottom of the package. Skin color depends on what the birds were fed, not on their freshness.

- Store poultry immediately after purchase in the refrigerator, covered, for no longer than two days or wrap in foil and freeze up to 6 months.

- Thaw frozen poultry in the refrigerator, not at room temperature. For a faster, still safe method, cover with cool (not hot) water. Change water frequently.

- Rinse chicken and pat dry with paper towels before cooking to remove any surface bacteria. Wash hands, cutting boards, and utensils with hot, soapy water to prevent cross-contamination when working with both raw poultry and other foods. (This rule applies to all raw meat.)

- Allow ¾ to 1 pound bone-in chicken per serving. A 3- to 3½-pound chicken or 1½ to 2 pounds boned and skinned chicken breasts will serve 4.

- Remove skin and extra fat, if desired, to reduce the fat content. (When the skin is removed, a marinade or sauce should be added to prevent chicken from drying out while cooking.)

- Cooking time for whole chicken is about 1¼ to 1½ hours, depending on size. Chicken pieces take about 1 hour, boneless chicken breasts about 30 minutes, bone in breasts take about 45 minutes. Chicken is done when meat is white and juices run clear when tested with a sharp knife inserted into the thickest part.

- Refrigerate leftover cooked poultry as soon as possible.

Orange–Hazelnut Chicken

Chicken breasts are dipped in fresh orange juice and then rolled in a delicious nut-crumb coating. They can be prepared ahead and baked just before serving. Add Caesar Salad, San Francisco Style (page 50), Orange, Rice, and Barley Pilaf (page 208), and Blueberry Pie (page 260) to complete the meal.

1 cup fine dry bread crumbs

1/4 cup finely chopped toasted hazelnuts or almonds (pages 58 or 78)

1/2 teaspoon salt

1/2 teaspoon dried thyme, crumbled

1/8 teaspoon freshly ground pepper

3 tablespoons chopped parsley

2 tablespoons butter or margarine

1/4 cup fresh orange juice

4 to 6 boned and skinned chicken breast halves

Sliced oranges, for garnish

Preheat oven to 350°F. On a piece of waxed paper mix crumbs, nuts, seasonings, and parsley.

In a small pan over medium heat melt butter and add orange juice.

Dip chicken, one piece at a time, in butter and juice mixture and then roll in crumb-nut mixture. Place in a lightly oiled or sprayed 7½- by 11¾-inch baking dish. Pour any leftover butter and juice mixture over breasts.

Bake, uncovered, until chicken is golden and crisp and meat is white in center when tested with a knife, about 35 minutes. Transfer to a plate and garnish with orange slices.

Chicken Breasts with Spinach Filling and Cheese-Taragon Sauce

SERVES 6 TO 8

These stuffed chicken breasts topped with Cheese-Tarragon Sauce make an impressive presentation. Serve with Acini di Pepe and Mushrooms (page 201) along with Broiled Tomato Slices (page 184) and a fruit salad. Include Toffee Nut Bars (page 284) for dessert.

2 tablespoons butter
   or margarine
½ cup diced yellow onion
½ cup diced red bell
   pepper
1 bag (6 ounces) spinach,
   stems removed, or
   1 cup (10 ounces)
   frozen spinach, thawed
   and squeezed dry
3 tablespoons water
   (if using fresh spinach)
½ teaspoon salt
⅛ teaspoon freshly
   ground pepper
¼ teaspoon dried
   tarragon, crumbled
Dash of nutmeg
6 to 8 boned and skinned
   chicken breast halves
½ cup grated Swiss cheese
⅓ cup dry white wine
Paprika
Cheese-Tarragon Sauce
   (recipe follows)

In a skillet melt butter over medium heat. Add onion and red pepper and sauté about 5 minutes. If using fresh spinach, place it in a large saucepan, add water, cover, and cook, tossing with a fork once or twice, until spinach wilts, about 2 to 3 minutes. Drain well and finely chop. If using frozen spinach, thaw and squeeze dry. Combine spinach with sautéed vegetables and season with salt, pepper, tarragon, and nutmeg, and mix well. Remove from heat.

Preheat oven to 375°F. Prepare chicken breasts. Rinse and pat dry with a paper towel. Place each breast between 2 pieces of waxed paper and flatten with a meat mallet until ¼ inch thick. Divide spinach filling among the 8 breasts and sprinkle with cheese. Lift edges over the filling and secure with toothpicks.

Place seam-side down in an oiled 7½- by 11¾-inch baking dish. Pour wine over. Sprinkle paprika on top.

Bake in the oven until chicken is tender and filling is heated through, about 35 minutes. Make Cheese-Tarragon Sauce. Transfer chicken to a platter. Add juices from pan to cheese sauce and top each breast with about 1 tablespoon of sauce. Pass remaining sauce in a bowl. Serve immediately.

Cheese-Tarragon Sauce

2 tablespoons butter or margarine
2 tablespoons flour
¼ teaspoon salt
⅛ teaspoon white pepper
¼ teaspoon dried tarragon, crumbled
1 cup chicken broth
¼ cup grated Swiss cheese
2 tablespoons dry white wine

In a saucepan over medium heat melt butter. Add flour, salt, pepper, and tarragon and stir until blended. Add broth slowly and cook until bubbly and thickened, stirring constantly, about 3 minutes. Reduce heat to low. Stir in cheese, wine, and juices from chicken and cook until cheese is melted, about 1 minute.

Makes about 1½ cups

Chicken Breasts Stuffed with Sun-Dried Tomatoes and Ricotta Cheese

SERVES 6

We had this entrée at one of our favorite restaurants in San Francisco. Here is my version. It is just as good—maybe better. Serve with butter lettuce and Homemade Ranch Dressing (page 53), Lemony Green Beans (page 166), and Cranberry Sorbet (page 285) for dessert. For a company dinner include Crab for Crackers (page 18) as an hors d'oeuvre.

¼ cup chopped dry sun-dried tomatoes (not packed in oil) (see notes)

1 cup boiling water

4 or 5 fresh basil leaves, chopped, or ¾ teaspoon dried basil (see notes)

3 green onions including some tender green tops, cut up

3 sprigs parsley

1 cup low-fat ricotta cheese

2 tablespoons freshly grated Parmesan cheese

¼ teaspoon salt

Freshly ground pepper to taste

Preheat oven to 350°F. In a small bowl or cup place sun-dried tomatoes. Add boiling water and let stand 10 minutes; then drain and dry. In food processor place tomatoes, basil, onions, and parsley. Process until chopped. Scrape down sides of bowl with spatula. Add cheeses and salt and process again until blended.

Loosen skin on chicken with a sharp knife or fingers to make a pocket. Remove any visible fat. Insert about 2 tablespoons of filling under the skin. Pull skin over filling. Place breasts in an oiled or lightly sprayed 9- by 13-inch baking dish. Brush tops of chicken with oil and sprinkle lightly with paprika.

6 bone-in chicken breast halves (3 to 3½ pounds), with skin
Vegetable oil, for brushing on chicken
Paprika
Fresh basil leaves, for garnish

Bake until chicken is lightly browned and juices run clear, about 1 hour. Baste with pan juices once while cooking. Garnish with basil leaves and serve immediately.

Notes:
• Sun-dried tomatoes can be purchased dried or packed in oil. Dry sun-dried tomatoes must be reconstituted: soak in boiling water to cover for 5 minutes, drain, and dry. Sun-dried tomatoes packed in oil are ready for use after being rinsed and patted dry.
• If using dried basil, increase parsley to 6 sprigs.

Cajun Blackened Chicken Breasts

Cajun cooking has found its way to other parts of the country and has become very popular. In this recipe the chicken breasts are highly seasoned and cooked quickly in a cast-iron skillet over high heat. (Turn on the fan and open the door.) Accompany with Orzo and Parmesan Cheese (page 202), hard rolls, and Garden Salad (page 52) with a dressing of your choice.

4 tablespoons butter or margarine, melted

6 boned and skinned chicken breast halves, flattened

3 tablespoons Cajun seasoning (recipe follows), or purchased Cajun seasoning

Place butter in a flat bowl. Dip chicken in butter and place on a plate. Sprinkle both sides with seasoning.

Preheat a cast-iron skillet over high heat until drops of water sizzle, about 5 minutes. Place chicken in skillet. Cook chicken until thoroughly browned on one side, about 4 minutes. Drizzle on remaining butter, turn with tongs and cook about 5 minutes longer. If skillet will not hold all chicken breasts at one time, cook in batches and transfer to a warm oven.

Cajun Seasoning

1 teaspoon garlic powder

1 teaspoon dried basil, crumbled

1 teaspoon dried thyme, crumbled

¼ teaspoon dried oregano, crumbled

1 tablespoon paprika

1 teaspoon celery salt

¼ teaspoon ground cayenne pepper

½ teaspoon white pepper

½ teaspoon onion powder

In a cup or small bowl combine all ingredients. Store any leftover seasoning in a spice jar with lid.

Makes about 2½ tablespoons

Note: This seasoning is also good on snapper. Follow the same cooking directions.

Chicken Breasts and Mushrooms with Rosemary and Mustard Sauce

SERVES 4

This is a delicious company dish that can be made ahead and then reheated at serving time. For a great beginning start with Party Salmon Mousse (page 20), serve with Wild Rice Plus (page 210), Tomato-Broccoli Cups (page 165), and Assorted Fruit with Honey-Yogurt Sauce (page 77) as a salad. Kahla Chocolate Ice Cream Torte (page 270) makes a grand ending.

3 tablespoons butter or margarine

6 boned and skinned chicken breast halves

Salt and freshly ground pepper to taste

6 green onions including some tender green tops, sliced

2 cups sliced mushrooms

¾ cup dry white wine

1 cup chicken broth

¼ teaspoon salt

1 tablespoon snipped rosemary, or ¾ teaspoon dried rosemary, crumbled

2 tablespoons Dijon mustard

2 tablespoons chopped parsley

Rosemary sprigs, for garnish

In a skillet melt 2 tablespoons butter over medium heat. Season chicken with salt and pepper. Cook chicken in skillet until well browned and no longer pink in the center, about 20 minutes, turning several times. Remove to a plate. Add remaining 1 tablespoon butter to skillet and sauté onion and mushrooms until soft, about 5 minutes. Remove and add to chicken. Add wine, broth, salt, and rosemary to pan; increase heat to medium-high and boil until liquid is reduced by about one-half, about 5 minutes. Whisk in mustard and parsley. Return chicken and mushrooms to pan and simmer over low heat to reheat, 5 to 10 minutes. Garnish with rosemary sprigs and serve immediately.

Baked Tarragon Chicken Breasts

Easy to make, but good enough for a company dinner, these chicken breasts are simply baked in a tasty sauce. Serve with Rice and Mushroom Pilaf (page 207) and California Salad and Tarragon-Sesame Seed Dressing (page 54). Include Fresh Peach Crisp (page 257) for dessert.

6 boned and skinned chicken breast halves

2 tablespoons butter or margarine

2 tablespoons Dijon mustard

3 tablespoons dry white wine

1 teaspoon lemon juice

1 tablespoon chopped fresh tarragon, or 1 teaspoon dry tarragon, crumbled

½ tablespoon salt

Freshly ground pepper to taste

Preheat oven to 350°F. Place chicken in a lightly oiled or sprayed 8- by 8-inch baking dish. In a small saucepan melt butter. Whisk in remaining ingredients. Pour over chicken. Bake, uncovered, until chicken is no longer pink in the center, about 35 minutes. Spoon sauce over chicken and serve immediately.

Baked Chicken Thighs with Lemon Sauce

This chicken bakes in a tasty sauce for an easy oven dish. Serve with a fruit salad, Sweet Onion and Rice Bake (page 182), asparagus, and Citrus-Nut Cake (page 276).

6 chicken thighs (1¾ to 2 pounds), skinned
Salt and pepper to taste
Paprika, for sprinkling on chicken
¼ cup lemon juice
½ cup chicken broth
2 tablespoons sherry or dry white wine
¼ teaspoon lemon zest
¼ teaspoon ground cloves
¼ cup firmly packed brown sugar
¼ teaspoon salt
2 teaspoons cornstarch

Preheat oven to 350°F. Place chicken in a lightly oiled or sprayed 7½- by 11¾-inch baking dish. Season with salt, pepper, and paprika.

In a small saucepan combine lemon juice, broth, sherry, lemon zest, cloves, brown sugar, salt, and cornstarch. Bring to a boil over medium-high heat and cook until mixture thickens slightly, stirring constantly, about 3 minutes.

Spoon sauce over chicken and bake until juices run clear, about 55 minutes. Baste with sauce and juices once while baking. Serve immediately.

Spanish Chicken with Olives

A great recipe that can be made in mere minutes. Serve Chunky Guacamole (page 24) and chips for an hors d'oeuvre. With the chicken offer plain rice or noodles to absorb the delicious sauce and a plate of sliced red onions, oranges, and cucumbers. Try Cashew Brownies (page 280) for dessert.

1 chicken (about 3½ pounds), cut into serving pieces
Salt and freshly ground pepper to taste
Tangy Beer-Tomato Sauce (recipe follows)
1 cup ripe olives, drained

Preheat oven to 350°F. Season chicken with salt and pepper. Place in a lightly oiled or sprayed 4-quart baking dish. Pour Tangy Beer-Tomato Sauce over chicken. Cover and bake until chicken juices run clear when tested with a knife, about 1 hour. Add olives and cook, uncovered, 5 minutes longer. Serve immediately.

Tangy Beer-Tomato Sauce

1 can (6 ounces) tomato paste
1 cup beer, allowed to go flat
¼ teaspoon salt
2 cloves garlic, minced
1 can (4 ounces) diced green chiles, drained

In a bowl whisk together all ingredients.

Makes about 2½ cups

Oven-Barbecued Chicken with Bacon

Make this easy oven dish at any time of the year. As the bacon cooks, it adds flavor and moisture to the chicken. For an oven dinner include baked potatoes and acorn squash.

1 yellow onion, separated
    into rings
1 chicken (3 to 3½
    pounds), cut into
    serving pieces
Barbecue Sauce (recipe
    follows)
6 bacon strips,
    cut into 2-inch pieces

Preheat oven to 350°F. In a lightly oiled or sprayed 9- by 13-inch baking dish place onion rings. Place chicken on top of onions. Spread Barbecue Sauce evenly over chicken and top with bacon pieces.

Bake, uncovered, until juices run clear when tested with a knife and bacon is crisp, about 1 hour. Baste once with sauce while baking.

Barbecue Sauce

½ cup catsup
¼ cup water
1 teaspoon Worcestershire
    sauce
1 teaspoon vinegar
1 tablespoon honey

In a small bowl combine all ingredients.

Makes about 1 cup

Baked Crunchy Coated Chicken

Chicken pieces are rolled in a flavorful coating and then baked in the oven. No browning is necessary. Serve with Romaine-Bacon-Apple Salad (page 56), Pasta and Grain Pilaf (page 203), Orange Broccoli (page 163), and Old-Fashioned Icebox Cookies (page 281).

½ cup plain nonfat yogurt

1 tablespoon Dijon mustard

½ teaspoon salt

Freshly ground pepper to taste

1 cup dried bread crumbs

¼ cup freshly grated Parmesan cheese

1 tablespoon sesame seeds

¼ teaspoon dried basil, crumbled

¼ teaspoon dried rosemary, crumbled

¼ teaspoon dried thyme, crumbled

¼ teaspoon paprika

¼ cup chopped parsley

1 chicken (3½ to 4 pounds), cut into serving pieces

Preheat oven to 350°F. In a pie plate mix yogurt, mustard, salt, and pepper. On a piece of waxed paper or on a plate combine remaining ingredients except chicken. Roll chicken pieces in yogurt mixture and then in crumb mixture.

Place in a lightly oiled or sprayed 9- by 13-inch baking dish. Bake until chicken turns white and coating is lightly browned, about 1 hour. Serve hot or cold.

Greek-Style Roasted Whole Chicken

SERVES **4** TO **6**

This seasoned chicken bakes in lemon juice along with its own juices for an easy oven dish. Bulgur and Almond Pilaf (page 204) and Greek Salad with Feta Cheese (page 49) go well with this entrée; Spiced Apple Crisp (page 258) makes a great ending.

1 whole chicken (about 3 1/2 pounds)
Salt and pepper to taste
1 lemon, halved
2 cloves garlic
1 sprig fresh oregano
Paprika
2 teaspoons oregano, crumbled
1/2 teaspoon salt
Freshly ground pepper to taste
1/2 cup crumbled feta cheese (optional)
Fresh oregano sprigs, for garnish

Preheat oven to 350°F. Place chicken breast-side up in a lightly oiled or sprayed 9- by 13-inch baking dish. Salt and pepper chicken cavity and tuck in 1/2 lemon, garlic, and oregano sprig. Pour juice of remaining 1/2 lemon over chicken, then sprinkle with paprika, oregano, salt, and pepper.

Roast, uncovered, until chicken is browned and juices run clear when tested with a knife, about 1 1/2 hours. If chicken becomes too brown, cover loosely with foil. Baste several times with juices while cooking.

Transfer to a warmed platter and cover loosely with foil for 10 minutes. Remove foil and slice into serving pieces. Sprinkle with feta cheese and garnish with oregano sprigs.

Family Night Chicken Stew

SERVES 6

This is a great dish to put in the oven and forget for two hours.
It makes a good family meal or informal supper for friends.
Serve with plain noodles or rice, to absorb the delicious sauce,
and a fresh fruit platter.

2½ pounds chicken pieces (drumsticks, thighs, and bone-in breast halves), skinned

1 yellow onion, quartered

3 carrots, cut into 1-inch pieces

3 celery stalks, cut into 1-inch pieces

1 red bell pepper, seeded, cut into 1-inch pieces

¼ cup quick-cooking tapioca

½ cup fine dry bread crumbs

½ pound whole mushrooms

1½ teaspoons salt

1 can (14½ ounces) whole tomatoes including juice, cut up

1 cup dry white wine

Preheat oven to 325°F. Combine all ingredients in a lightly oiled or sprayed 4-quart casserole. Bake, covered, for 2 hours. Remove lid, stir, and bake, uncovered, 20 minutes longer.

Chicken Roll-Ups, Mexican Style

SERVES 4 TO 6

Chicken breasts stuffed with chiles and cheese and rolled in crushed tortilla chips have a south-of-the-border flavor. Serve with Avocado Mexican Salad (page 60), Pink Rice (page 206), and warm flour tortillas (see note), and chocolate ice cream for dessert.

6 to 8 boned and skinned chicken breast halves

Salt and freshly ground pepper to taste

3 or 4 canned whole green chiles, seeded, rinsed, split, and cut in half lengthwise

6 to 8 strips (1 by 3 inches) Monterey Jack cheese

¾ cup buttermilk

1 cup crushed tortilla chips

Preheat oven to 350°F. Place each chicken breast between 2 pieces of waxed paper and pound with a meat mallet until ¼-inch thick. Season lightly with salt and pepper. Place 1 chile half and 1 cheese strip in the middle of each chicken breast. Roll up each breast piece from narrow end and secure in place with a toothpick.

Pour buttermilk into a pie plate. On a large piece of waxed paper spread tortilla chips. Dip each rolled breast first in buttermilk and then roll in chips to coat evenly. Arrange in a lightly oiled or sprayed 7½- by 11¾-inch baking dish.

Bake, uncovered, until chicken is golden brown and juices run clear, about 45 minutes. Serve immediately.

Note: Wrap warm tortillas in a napkin to keep them from drying out.

Chicken, Black Bean, and Tortilla Casserole

SERVES 6

A terrific combination of favorite ingredients that is easy to assemble. Serve with Chunky Guacamole (page 24), melon slices, and Buttermilk Chocolate Cake (page 278) with vanilla ice cream for dessert.

1 tablespoon vegetable oil

1 large yellow onion, chopped

1/2 green pepper, seeded and chopped

2 cloves garlic, minced

1 can (14 1/2 ounces) tomatoes including juices, slightly puréed

1/2 cup prepared salsa

1 teaspoon cumin

3/4 teaspoon salt and freshly ground pepper to taste

1/2 teaspoon oregano, crumbled

2 cans (15 ounces each) black beans, drained and rinsed

2 to 3 cups cubed, cooked chicken breasts

8 corn tortillas

4 cups grated Monterey Jack cheese

TOPPINGS

Plain nonfat yogurt

Sour cream

Avocado slices

Sliced green onions

Chopped olives

In a large skillet warm oil over medium heat. Add onion, green pepper, and garlic and sauté until vegetables are soft, about 5 minutes. Add tomatoes, salsa, cumin, salt, pepper, and oregano and mix well. Stir in beans and chicken.

Preheat oven to 350°F. In a lightly oiled or sprayed 4-quart casserole or large oval baking dish spread one-third of the bean and chicken mixture over the bottom. Top with 4 tortillas and sprinkle with 1 cup cheese. Add another one-third of the bean and chicken mixture and 1 cup cheese. Top with 4 tortillas and 1 cup cheese. Add remaining bean and chicken mixture. Cover and bake until bubbly, about 40 minutes.

Uncover and sprinkle with remaining cheese and cook 10 minutes longer. Let stand 5 minutes before serving. Serve with toppings.

Chicken and Vegetable Stir-fry

Stir-fried dishes are healthful, economical, and easy to prepare. Have all ingredients and serving dishes ready before you begin. The marinated chicken and vegetables are quickly tossed in a small amount of oil until the chicken is done and the vegetables are tender crisp. Serve with plain rice, Oriental Cucumbers with Soy Dressing (recipe follows), and fortune cookies for a fun dessert.

¼ cup soy sauce

3 tablespoons dry white wine

1 tablespoon cornstarch

1 tablespoon freshly grated ginger, or ½ teaspoon ground ginger

1 clove garlic, minced

4 chicken breast halves, about 1 pound, cut into ¾-inch pieces

3 tablespoons vegetable oil

½ red bell pepper, cut into bite-sized pieces

½ pound mushrooms, sliced

6 green onions including some tender green tops, sliced

In a bowl stir together soy sauce, wine, cornstarch, ginger, and garlic. Add chicken and mix to coat well. Cover and marinate in refrigerator several hours. Bring to room temperature before cooking.

Heat a wok or heavy skillet over medium-high heat. Add 1 tablespoon oil. When oil sizzles, remove chicken from marinade with a slotted spoon and add to wok. Reserve marinade. Stir-fry chicken, constantly stirring and tossing until chicken turns white, about 4 minutes. Remove to a plate.

Add remaining oil and when it is hot, stir-fry vegetables until tender crisp, about 5 minutes.

Return chicken to wok along with remaining marinade. Stir until sauce thickens and all ingredients are heated through, 1 to 2 minutes longer. Transfer to a warm platter and serve immediately with rice.

Oriental Cucumbers with Soy Dressing

2 large or 3 medium cucumbers, peeled and thinly sliced
4 green onions including some tender green tops, sliced
Soy Dressing (recipe follows)

Toss cucumbers and onions in Soy Dressing, cover, and marinate several hours or overnight, stirring occasionally. Drain before serving.

Serves 6

Soy Dressing

1/2 cup rice vinegar
2 tablespoons water
1 teaspoon sugar
2 teaspoons soy sauce
1/4 teaspoon salt
Freshly ground pepper to taste

In a bowl large enough to hold cucumbers combine all ingredients.

Makes about 1/2 cup

Chicken Enchiladas

Here is a fun, informal, Mexican-inspired recipe for chicken enchiladas that may be served with other typical Mexican dishes: Baked Black Bean Dip (page 23) or Chunky Guacamole (page 24) and chips, Orange, Cucumber, and Jícama Salad with Lime-Cumin Dressing (page 74), Pink Rice (page 206), refried beans, and Flan (Crème Caramel) (page 266) for dessert.

4 boned and skinned chicken breast halves

¼ teaspoon salt

Enchilada Sauce (recipe follows), or 3 cans (10 ounces each) enchilada sauce (2 mild, 1 hot)

1 package (12) corn tortillas, at room temperature

8 ounces Monterey Jack cheese, grated (about 2 cups)

½ cup light sour cream

8 green onions including some tender green tops, sliced

8 ounces Cheddar cheese, grated (about 2 cups)

½ cup ripe olives (optional)

Light sour cream or plain nonfat yogurt, as an accompaniment

In a saucepan cover chicken with water and add salt. Bring to a boil, then reduce heat to low and cook, covered, until chicken turns white, about 10 minutes. Remove chicken to a plate to cool. When cool, cut into ½-inch-wide strips. Set aside.

Meanwhile, make the Enchilada Sauce.

Preheat oven to 350°F. Spread ¼ cup Enchilada Sauce in the bottom of a 9- by 13-inch oiled or lightly sprayed baking dish or large decorative casserole. Dip one tortilla in hot enchilada sauce for a few seconds to soften. Remove with tongs and lay flat on a plate. Immediately add another tortilla to sauce.

Place several chicken strips in the center of the tortilla on the plate. Top with a row of Jack cheese, 2 teaspoons sour cream, and a few chopped onions. Roll up and place seam-side down in baking dish. Repeat procedure with remaining tortillas. Pour remaining sauce evenly over tortillas. Sprinkle with Cheddar cheese and dot with olives. Bake, uncovered, until hot and bubbly, 30 to 35 minutes. Serve immediately with sour cream or yogurt.

Note: Can be made ahead and refrigerated. Bring to room temperature before baking.

Enchilada Sauce

1 can (15 ounces) tomato sauce

1 can (6 ounces) tomato paste

3/4 cup water

1 can (10 1/2 ounces) beef broth, undiluted

1/4 teaspoon ground cumin

1/4 teaspoon garlic powder

2 teaspoons chili powder (or more to taste)

1/4 teaspoon paprika

1/2 teaspoon dried oregano, crumbled

1/4 teaspoon salt

2 to 3 drops Tabasco sauce

Freshly ground pepper to taste

In a saucepan blend all ingredients. Simmer, over low heat, uncovered, for 5 minutes.

Makes about 4 cups

Make-Ahead Chicken or Turkey Casserole

SERVES 6

This casserole is for the cook who wants to avoid last-minute preparation. It can be made ahead (see note) and baked later. Serve with Orange Broccoli (page 163), Pear Salad with Blue Cheese Topping (page 75), and for dessert, Citrus-Nut Cake (page 276).

2 cups chicken broth or water

1 cup long-grain white rice

2 to 3 tablespoons butter or margarine

1/2 pound mushrooms, sliced

1/2 red bell pepper, seeded and chopped

2 tablespoons chopped yellow onion

1/4 cup slivered almonds

1/4 cup chopped parsley

1 tablespoon chopped fresh basil, or 3/4 teaspoon dried basil, crumbled

3 to 4 cups cubed cooked chicken or turkey breast

Parmesan Cheese Sauce (recipe follows)

Salt and freshly ground pepper, to taste

In a saucepan bring broth to a boil. Add rice, reduce temperature to low and cook, covered, until liquid is absorbed, about 20 minutes. Place in a lightly oiled or sprayed 4-quart casserole.

While the rice is cooking, make Parmesan Cheese Sauce and set aside.

Preheat oven to 350°F. In a skillet over medium heat melt butter. Add mushrooms, bell pepper, onion, and almonds. Sauté until vegetables are soft, about 5 minutes. Stir in parsley and basil. Add to rice in the casserole along with chicken and Parmesan Cheese Sauce and mix well. Season with salt and pepper. Bake, covered, until bubbly, about 45 minutes. Serve immediately.

Note: If made ahead, cover and refrigerate. Bring to room temperature before baking.

Parmesan Cheese Sauce

3 tablespoons butter or
   margarine
3 tablespoons flour
1/4 teaspoon salt
3/4 cup chicken broth
1 cup milk
2 tablespoons white wine
3 tablespoons freshly
   grated Parmesan
   cheese
1/2 cup light sour cream

In a saucepan over medium heat melt butter. Add flour and salt and stir until blended. Add broth and stir until slightly thickened. Add milk, wine, and Parmesan cheese, and stir until smooth and flavors are blended, about 2 minutes. Remove from heat and whisk in sour cream.

Makes about 2 cups

Turkey Meatballs

Freshly ground, lean turkey is readily available in the meat section of most supermarkets. The sun-dried tomatoes add flavor and color. Serve with Savory Brown Rice (page 212), seasonal fruit, and Chocolate Fudge Pie with Hazelnut Whipped Cream (page 265) for dessert.

1 cup water
1/2 cup chopped dry sun-dried tomatoes
1 1/2 pounds ground turkey
1/4 cup finely chopped yellow onion
1 clove garlic, minced
1 large egg, beaten
1/2 cup fresh bread crumbs
1/4 cup milk
1/4 cup chopped parsley
1/4 teaspoon salt
1/2 teaspoon poultry seasoning
Freshly ground pepper to taste
1 cup chicken broth
2 tablespoons white wine
2 tablespoons flour
Salt and freshly ground pepper to taste

In a small pan over high heat bring water to a boil. Add tomatoes. Remove from heat and let stand 10 minutes. Drain and dry.

Preheat oven to 375°F. In a large bowl mix all ingredients (including tomatoes) but not chicken broth, wine, and flour. Shape into 1½-inch meatballs. Place on a lightly oiled or sprayed baking sheet with a rim. Bake until browned, about 15 minutes, stirring once.

Meanwhile, in a saucepan whisk broth and wine with flour. Place over medium-high heat and bring to a boil. Whisk until thickened. Season with salt and pepper. Add meatballs and juices and simmer until flavors are blended, about 5 minutes. Serve immediately.

The Fish Market

Fish appears more often on today's
menus because of the health benefits
that are now widely recognized.
Nutritionists recommend two or three
servings a week as a good source
of protein and other nutrients. Current
research indicates that the omega-3
fatty acids found in fish oils lower
cholesterol levels and may reduce
the risk of heart disease.

Aquaculture (fish farming) has
become a big industry, especially on
the West Coast, resulting in an
expanded market. With
air transportation,
fresh seafood is now
regularly available in
most parts of our country.
However, coastal areas still
have the advantage of
a larger supply and selection.

Fish Basics

When buying fish and seafood, rely on a fish market with a good reputation. Fish should smell fresh and mild with no offensive odor. Fillets and steaks should be moist and firm and look freshly cut. Whole fish should have bright skin, clear eyes, pinkish gills, and scales tightly attached.

Fish and seafood are highly perishable and should be refrigerated immediately after purchase. If this is not possible, request that your fish be wrapped with ice.

Allow ⅓ to ½ pound per person.

Cook fish and seafood the day of purchase. Before cooking, wash and pat fish dry with a paper towel to remove surface bacteria. To refresh, if desired, dip in cold acidulated water (water to which a small amount of vinegar, lemon, or lime juice has been added) and then dry thoroughly.

Fish is naturally tender and full of flavor and is very adaptable to all methods of cooking. Preparation is quick and easy.

Marinades are often used to enhance the flavor. Fish should not, however, be left for longer than 15 minutes in an acid-based marinade because the juice will begin to "cook" the fish.

Fish should be cooked quickly at high heat. A general rule is to cook most fish 8 to 10 minutes per 1 inch of thickness measured at the thickest part. To test for doneness, prod with a fork and, when the fish begins to flake, it is done. Overcooking produces dry fish and a loss of flavor and nutrients.

Serve fish lightly seasoned with a squeeze of lemon or lime, salt, and pepper, or with a complementary sauce. Always serve on warm plates immediately after cooking.

Red Snapper with Salsa

Fresh Pacific red snapper or rockfish is a popular choice because of its distinctive flavor and economical price. The snapper baked with an onion and salsa topping goes well with Roasted New Potatoes (page 174). Follow with Blueberry-Cranberry Crisp (page 259) for dessert.

1½ to 2 pounds Pacific red snapper fillets

2 tablespoons fresh lemon juice

Salt and freshly ground pepper to taste

½ yellow onion, sliced

1 cup Fresh Tomato Salsa (page 13), or prepared salsa

1 lime, cut into wedges, for garnish

Preheat oven to 400°F. In a lightly oiled or sprayed 7½- by 11¾-inch glass baking dish, place snapper dark side down. Sprinkle with lemon juice, salt, and pepper. Place onion slices on top of fish.

Spoon salsa evenly over onion slices. Bake until fish flakes when tested with a fork, about 20 to 25 minutes. Garnish with lime slices and serve immediately.

Citrus Salmon Steaks

Fresh Pacific salmon has a superb, distinctive flavor and is well known throughout the country. Marinated with a simple citrus marinade and served with Lemon-Caper-Dill Sauce, it is an outstanding main course. Add Caesar Salad, San Francisco Style (page 50), Roasted New Potatoes (page 174), fresh peas, and Deep-dish Berry Pie (page 262) for dessert.

4 salmon steaks
  (1½ to 2 pounds)
Citrus Marinade (recipe
  follows)
Lemon-Caper-Dill Sauce
  (recipe follows)

Place salmon in a glass baking dish, pour marinade over, and turn steaks to coat. Marinate for 15 minutes at room temperature.

Prepare broiler. Remove steaks from marinade and place on broiler rack. Broil until lightly browned, about 4 to 5 minutes on each side, brushing with remaining marinade. Transfer to a platter and serve immediately. Pass the Lemon-Caper-Dill Sauce in a bowl.

Citrus Marinade

1 tablespoon vegetable oil
2 tablespoons fresh lemon
  juice
2 tablespoons fresh orange
  juice
1 teaspoon Worcestershire
  sauce
Salt and freshly ground
  pepper to taste

In a small bowl stir together marinade ingredients.

Makes about ¼ cup

Lemon–Caper–Dill Sauce

½ cup light mayonnaise

¼ cup plain nonfat yogurt

1 tablespoon fresh lemon juice

1 tablespoon snipped fresh dill, or
½ teaspoon dried dill weed, crumbled

1 teaspoon drained capers

¼ teaspoon salt

¼ teaspoon sugar

Freshly ground pepper to taste

In a small bowl mix all ingredients together. Cover and refrigerate unless using immediately. Serve at room temperature.

Makes about ¾ cup

Baked Salmon

Salmon lends itself to almost any cooking method, but baked salmon is always a favorite. Serve with Spinach, Pear, and Walnut Salad with Raspberry Vinaigrette (page 48), fresh asparagus, and Apricot and Blueberry Flan (page 267).

Mayonnaise as needed
1 piece whole salmon, about 3 pounds
Salt and freshly ground pepper to taste
1 yellow onion, sliced
1 lemon, sliced
Parsley sprigs
Rémoulade Sauce (recipe follows) or Pesto Mayonnaise (page 117)

Preheat oven to 425°F. Spread a thin layer of mayonnaise over the bottom of a 7½- by 11¾-inch glass baking dish or foil pan. Place salmon on top of mayonnaise. Season cavity with salt and pepper and tuck in onion, half of lemon slices, and a few parsley sprigs. Spread mayonnaise generously on top of salmon and add remaining lemon slices.

Bake until fish flakes when tested with a fork, 8 to 10 minutes per inch of thickness of fish, about 1 hour.

Serve immediately with Rémoulade Sauce or Pesto Mayonnaise.

Rémoulade Sauce

A complementary sauce for most seafood.

3/4 cup light mayonnaise
1 tablespoon lemon juice
1 teaspoon Dijon mustard
2 sprigs parsley
2 green onions including some tender green tops, cut up
1 tablespoon capers, drained
1/4 teaspoon salt
1/4 teaspoon dried tarragon, crumbled
Dash of Tabasco sauce
Freshly ground pepper to taste

In a food processor place all ingredients and process until smooth. Cover and refrigerate until ready to serve. Serve at room temperature.

Makes about 3/4 cup

Sesame Snapper

Sesame seeds impart an unusual flavor and add a crunchy coating. Serve with Cashew Coleslaw (page 61), Broiled Tomato Slices (page 184), and Orange, Rice, and Barley Pilaf (page 208). End the meal with Blueberry Pie (page 260).

¼ cup sesame seeds

1 cup fine dried bread crumbs

½ cup skim milk, for dipping fish

1½ pounds red snapper or other white fish

Juice of 1 lemon

¼ teaspoon salt

⅛ teaspoon pepper

2 tablespoons butter or margarine, melted

Tartar Sauce (page 127)

Preheat oven to 425°F. Combine sesame seeds and bread crumbs on a baking sheet and bake until golden brown, about 3 minutes, stirring once.

Pour milk into pie plate. Dip snapper into milk and then coat both sides evenly with crumb mixture. Arrange in a 7½- by 11¾-inch lightly oiled or sprayed baking dish. Sprinkle lemon juice over fish and season with salt and pepper. Drizzle butter over fish.

Bake until fish flakes when tested with a fork, 10 to 12 minutes. Transfer to a warmed platter and serve immediately, accompanied by Tartar Sauce.

Baked Halibut with Cashew—Crumb Topping

SERVES 4

Low in fat, firm in texture, and mild in flavor, halibut is always a popular choice. The crunchy cashew topping makes an appealing presentation. Serve with Cucumber and Red Onion Salad with Dill Dressing (page 64), Steamed Spinach and Garlic (page 183), Pasta and Grain Pilaf (page 203), and fresh berries for dessert.

1 tablespoon vegetable oil

1 1/2 to 2 pounds halibut steak or fillet

3/4 cup dry bread crumbs

2 tablespoons freshly grated Parmesan cheese

3 tablespoons chopped parsley

2 tablespoons chopped cashew nuts

1 tablespoon fresh snipped tarragon, or 1/2 teaspoon dried tarragon, crumbled

1 teaspoon lemon zest

1/2 teaspoon paprika

Freshly ground pepper to taste

Lemon wedges, for garnish

Preheat oven to 425°F. Place oil in a 9- by 13-inch glass baking dish. Add halibut and turn to coat with oil on both sides.

In a small bowl stir together remaining ingredients except lemon wedges. Press crumb mixture on top of halibut.

Bake until fish flakes when tested with a fork and top is golden, 10 to 12 minutes.

Serve immediately with lemon wedges.

Baked Sole with Bacon Topping

The crumbled bacon imparts a salty accent to the mild, delicate flavor of sole. Serve with a tossed green salad with Italian Dressing (page 56), parslied new potatoes, and Orange Broccoli (page 163). Complete the meal with lime sherbet for an easy going menu.

1 1/2 to 2 pounds sole or other white fish

2 tablespoons butter or margarine, melted

3 tablespoons fresh lemon juice

1/2 teaspoon salt

1/4 teaspoon freshly ground pepper

1/4 pound bacon, fried until crisp, crumbled

1 tablespoon chopped fresh chives, or sliced green onion tops

Preheat oven to 375°F. Place fish in a lightly oiled or sprayed 7 1/2- by 11 3/4-inch baking dish. In a small bowl combine butter, lemon juice, salt, and pepper and pour over fish.

Bake until fish flakes when tested with a fork, about 10 minutes. Transfer to a warmed platter and sprinkle with bacon and chives. Serve immediately.

Sole with Yogurt Topping

This easy to prepare oven fish dish is especially pleasing for an informal dinner. Serve a garden salad with Reed's Own Dressing (page 73), fresh green beans, Plank Potatoes with Parmesan Topping (page 173), and Cran-Applesauce (page 157).

1 1/2 to 2 pounds sole or other white fish

Salt and freshly ground pepper to taste

1/2 cup plain nonfat yogurt

2 tablespoons light mayonnaise

2 drops Tabasco sauce

1 tablespoon Dijon mustard

1/2 teaspoon Worcestershire sauce

1/4 teaspoon dried dill

4 green onions including some tender green tops, sliced

Freshly grated Parmesan cheese, for sprinkling on top

Paprika, for sprinkling on top

Preheat oven to 375°F. Place fish in a lightly oiled or sprayed 9- by 13-inch baking dish. Season with salt and pepper. In a small bowl mix together remaining ingredients, except onions and Parmesan cheese, and spread over fish.

Bake, uncovered, 10 minutes. Sprinkle onions, Parmesan cheese, and paprika over fish. Bake until fish flakes when tested with a fork, about 5 minutes longer. Serve immediately.

Broiled Swordfish with Fresh Peach–Avocado Salsa

SERVES 4

The flavor of swordfish is enhanced by this refreshing Fresh Peach-Avocado Salsa. Serve with Sauté of Summer Peas and Mushrooms (page 171), Pasta and Grain Pilaf (page 203), sliced tomatoes and cucumbers, and Lemon Drop Cookies (page 282).

1½ to 2 pounds swordfish fillets
1 tablespoon vegetable oil
2 tablespoons lemon juice
Salt and pepper to taste
Fresh Peach-Avocado Salsa (recipe follows)

Preheat oven to broil. Brush swordfish steaks lightly with oil and lemon juice. Place on broiler pan and broil until lightly browned, 4 to 5 minutes on each side. Season with salt and pepper. Serve immediately with Fresh Peach-Avocado Salsa.

Fresh Peach–Avocado Salsa

Salsa is not always tomato based; it can be a combination of vegetables or fruits and served as a relish.

1 large avocado, peeled, pitted, and chopped
1 large fresh peach, peeled, pitted, and chopped (see note)
3 tablespoons minced red onion
1 tablespoon chopped fresh basil, or ¾ teaspoon dried basil, crumbled
1 teaspoon sugar
¼ cup red wine vinegar

In a small bowl stir together all ingredients. Cover and refrigerate several hours. Serve at room temperature.

Note: If fresh peaches are not available, omit sugar and use drained, canned peaches.

Makes about 1 cup

Broiled Lemony Tuna with Pesto Mayonnaise

SERVES 4

Tuna, a full-flavored, firm fish, will retain its fresh flavor when brushed with this lemony sauce and broiled quickly. Serve with Pasta with Red Bell Pepper, Mushrooms, and Zucchini (page 198) and Sour Cream Lemon Pie (page 264) to round out the menu.

Juice of 1 lemon
1 tablespoon dry white wine
1 tablespoon Dijon mustard
1 tablespoon melted butter or margarine
1½ to 2 pounds tuna fillets
Salt and freshly ground pepper
Pesto Mayonnaise (recipe follows)

Preheat broiler. In a small bowl combine lemon juice, wine, mustard, and butter. Place fish on broiler pan. Brush with half of the lemon mixture. Broil 6 minutes on one side. Turn, brush with remaining lemon mixture, and broil until fish begins to flake easily when tested with a fork, about 5 minutes longer. Season with salt and pepper. Serve immediately. Pass the Pesto Mayonnaise in a separate bowl.

Pesto Mayonnaise

This sauce is also good on pasta.

¼ cup Basil Pesto (page 193) or purchased pesto
¼ cup light mayonnaise
1 teaspoon lemon juice

In a small bowl stir together all ingredients. Serve at room temperature.

Makes about ¾ cup

Herbed Tuna with Savory White Beans

Fresh tuna with white beans is a popular combination often served in restaurants. Add a tossed green salad with Sevé French Dressing (page 53), warm French bread, and sherbet for a satisfying meal.

MARINADE
¼ cup olive oil
2 tablespoons fresh lemon juice
1 clove garlic, minced
4 fresh basil leaves, chopped, or ½ teaspoon dried basil, crumbled
1 teaspoon chopped fresh rosemary, or ¼ teaspoon dried rosemary, crumbled

Tuna steaks (about 1½ to 2 pounds)
Salt and freshly ground pepper to taste
Savory White Beans (recipe follows)
Parsley sprigs, for garnish

In a small bowl mix marinade ingredients. Place steaks in a glass baking dish and pour marinade over. Cover and marinate 15 minutes at room temperature.

Prepare broiler. Remove steaks from marinade and place on broiler pan. Broil 4 to 5 minutes on each side or until fish begins to flake when tested with a fork. Brush with reserved marinade. Season with salt and pepper.

Serve on top of a bed of beans. Garnish with parsley and serve immediately.

Savory White Beans

1 1/2 cups Great Northern beans, sorted and rinsed

10 cups water

1 bay leaf

1/2 cup chopped yellow onion

2 cloves garlic, minced

2 tablespoons vegetable oil

1 large tomato, seeded, diced, and drained

5 fresh basil leaves, slivered, or 1/2 teaspoon dried basil, crumbled

1/4 teaspoon dried thyme, crumbled

1/2 teaspoon salt

Freshly ground pepper to taste

1/4 cup chopped parsley

In a large saucepan place beans, 5 cups water, and bay leaf. Boil for 2 minutes. Remove from heat, cover, and let stand for 1 hour.

Drain and add 5 cups fresh water. With lid slightly tilted, simmer over medium-low heat until beans are tender, about 1 hour. Remove bay leaf and discard. Drain beans, leaving about 1 tablespoon liquid in pan along with beans.

In a small skillet over medium heat, sauté onions and garlic in oil until soft, about 5 minutes. Add tomato, basil, thyme, salt, and pepper to the skillet and cook 2 to 3 minutes longer. Add tomato mixture and parsley to beans and mix well. Reduce heat and cover. Keep warm until serving time.

Serves 4 to 6 as a side dish

Note: Do not add salt until the end of the cooking period as it will toughen the beans.

Tangy Baked Shrimp

This is an easy way to prepare shrimp. Serve with fluffy white rice, California Salad with Tarragon-Sesame Seed Dressing (page 54), Roasted Vegetables (page 172), and ice cream and Berry Sauce (page 288) for dessert.

½ cup beer, allowed to go flat
1 tablespoon vegetable oil
2 cloves garlic, minced
2 teaspoons chili powder
1 teaspoon cumin
2 drops Tabasco sauce
¼ teaspoon salt
Freshly ground pepper to taste
1¼ pounds large shrimp, peeled and deveined
¼ cup chopped parsley

In a 9- by 13-inch baking dish mix all ingredients except shrimp and parsley. Add shrimp and stir to coat. Marinate 1 hour, at room temperature, turning occasionally.

Preheat oven to 425°F. In the same dish, bake shrimp with marinade until shrimp turns pink, about 10 minutes.

Spoon shrimp and some of sauce over rice. Sprinkle with parsley. Serve immediately.

Shrimp in Lime–Garlic Sauce

This was the way shrimp was prepared for us when we were guests at a villa in Puerto Vallarto, Mexico. The sharp lime juice emphasizes the flavor of the shrimp. Serve on a bed of spinach along with Rice and Mushroom Pilaf (page 207) and Flan (page 266) for dessert.

1 bag (6 ounces) prewashed spinach, stems removed

Salt and freshly ground pepper to taste

3 tablespoons vegetable oil

6 cloves garlic, coarsely chopped

16 large shrimp, shelled and deveined

3 tablespoons lime juice

½ teaspoon salt

Freshly ground pepper to taste

Cook spinach with a small amount of water in a large covered saucepan over high heat until wilted, about 2 minutes. Toss with a fork once or twice while cooking. Drain well, pressing out excess water. Add salt and pepper and place on a platter and keep warm.

In a large skillet over medium-high heat, warm the oil. Add garlic and sauté 1 minute.

Add shrimp and sauté until shrimp turn pink, about 2 minutes longer. Add lime juice, salt, and pepper and mix well. Cook 1 minute longer. Serve immediately over spinach.

Shrimp, Scallop, and Mushroom Sauté

A colorful and delicious combination of seafood and vegetables in a flavorful sauce. Mesclun Salad with Feta Cheese and Walnuts and Balsamic Vinaigrette (page 55), Pasta and Grain Pilaf (page 203), and Blueberry-Cranberry Crisp (page 259) go well with this entrée.

2 tablespoons butter or margarine

¾ pound large scallops, halved

¾ pound medium shrimp, shelled and deveined

6 green onions including some tender green tops, sliced

2 cloves garlic, chopped

½ red bell pepper, seeded and chopped

2 cups sliced mushrooms

¼ cup dry white wine

1 teaspoon Dijon mustard

1 teaspoon lemon juice

Salt and freshly ground pepper to taste

2 tablespoons chopped parsley

In a skillet melt butter over medium heat. Add scallops and sauté until they turn opaque, about 3 minutes. Add shrimp and sauté until they turn pink, about 3 minutes. With a slotted spoon, remove scallops and shrimp to a plate.

Add onions, garlic, bell pepper, and mushrooms and sauté until vegetables are tender, about 5 minutes. (Add more butter if necessary.) Stir in wine, mustard, lemon juice, salt, and pepper and cook until liquid is slightly reduced, 2 to 3 minutes. Return scallops and shrimp to sauce and cook until reheated and flavors are blended, about 5 minutes longer. Stir in parsley and serve immediately.

Spicy Seafood Stew

The seafood in this recipe may vary according to choice and availability. Serve with warm baguette slices.

3 to 4 tablespoons butter or margarine

1 small yellow onion, chopped

3 cloves garlic, minced

3 tablespoons flour

1/2 teaspoon curry powder

1/2 teaspoon ground cloves

2 tablespoons brown sugar

1/8 teaspoon saffron, crumbled

1 teaspoon salt

Freshly ground pepper to taste

1 can (46 ounces) tomato juice

1/4 teaspoon Tabasco sauce

1 can (6 1/2 ounces) minced clams including juice

1/4 cup dry white wine

1/4 cup chopped parsley

1/2 pound (about 20) medium shrimp, peeled and deveined

1/2 pound crab meat

1/2 pound scallops

1 1/2 pounds white fish, cut into bite-sized pieces

In a large saucepan melt butter over medium heat. Add onion and garlic and sauté until tender, about 5 minutes. Stir in flour and blend. Add curry, cloves, sugar, saffron, salt, and pepper and mix well.

Whisk in tomato juice and Tabasco and bring to a boil, stirring constantly.

Reduce heat, add clams and juice, wine, parsley, and seafood. Simmer, uncovered, until seafood is cooked and flavors are blended, 10 to 15 minutes. Serve immediately in large bowls.

Crab and Shrimp Cakes

These cakes, a combination of the two most popular shellfish topped with Roasted Red Pepper Aïoli, make an easy main course or appetizer. Add Spinach Salad with Mushrooms, Blue Cheese, and Bacon (page 57), fresh asparagus, and Cashew Brownies (page 280) with ice cream.

1 large egg

8 ounces shelled cooked crab, flaked and picked over

8 ounces cooked small shrimp, chopped

2 green onions including some tender green tops, finely chopped

1 cup crushed saltines (about 26)

1/4 cup light mayonnaise

1 teaspoon Worcestershire sauce

Dash of Tabasco sauce

1/4 teaspoon salt

1/4 teaspoon dry mustard

1 tablespoon butter or margarine

1 tablespoon vegetable oil

Roasted Red Pepper Aïoli (recipe follows)

In a bowl beat egg. Add remaining ingredients, except butter and oil, and mix thoroughly. Shape mixture into 8 cakes about ½-inch thick. (If serving for an appetizer, make 12 small cakes.)

In a large frying pan, melt half the butter with half the oil over medium heat. Fry 4 cakes until lightly browned, about 4 minutes on each side. Remove to a plate and keep warm. Add remaining butter and oil and fry the remaining cakes. Serve immediately with Roasted Red Pepper Aïoli.

Roasted Red Pepper Aïoli

1 roasted red bell pepper
  (page 8), cut up
2 cloves garlic, cut up
2 teaspoons red wine
  vinegar
1/4 teaspoon salt
1 cup light mayonnaise

In food processor chop roasted red pepper and garlic and then add the remaining ingredients and process until smooth. Cover and chill. Serve at room temperature.

Makes about 1 cup

Sautéed Almond Oysters with Two Sauces

The oysters in this recipe are rolled in a nutty crust and then quickly sautéed. A quick blanching firms them up and makes them easier to handle. Serve with Romaine-Bacon-Apple Salad (page 56), a green vegetable, Sweet Onion and Rice Bake (page 182), and Deep-dish Berry Pie (page 262).

3 cups water

2 dozen shucked oysters, rinsed

2 tablespoons milk

1 egg

1/2 teaspoon salt

1/4 teaspoon oregano, crumbled

2/3 cup crushed saltines (about 20)

3 tablespoons chopped almonds

2 tablespoons chopped parsley

1/4 cup butter

Lemon wedges, for garnish

Tartar Sauce (recipe follows)

Red Sauce (recipe follows)

In a saucepan over high heat bring water to a boil. Add oysters and blanch 3 minutes. Drain and pat dry.

In a bowl mix milk, egg, salt, and oregano. On a piece of waxed paper combine crackers, almonds, and parsley. Dip oysters in egg mixture, then roll in cracker crumb-nut mixture.

In a skillet melt butter over medium or medium-high heat. Sauté oysters in batches until golden and firm, 4 to 5 minutes on each side. Remove to a platter and keep warm. Serve with Tartar Sauce or Red Sauce.

Tartar Sauce

2 fresh parsley sprigs,
   cut up
2 green onions including
   some tender green
   tops, cut up
1 clove garlic, halved
1 sweet pickle, cut up
1/2 teaspoon Dijon
   mustard
1 teaspoon fresh lemon
   juice
Dash of Worcestershire
   sauce
1/4 teaspoon salt
1 cup mayonnaise

In food processor, combine parsley, onions, garlic, and pickle. Process until chopped. Add all remaining ingredients and process to blend. Transfer to a small bowl, cover, and refrigerate until serving, or up to 3 or 4 days. Serve at room temperature.

Note: For a quick tartar sauce, mix together 1 cup light mayonnaise, 2 tablespoons sweet pickle relish, and 1 teaspoon lemon juice.

Makes about 1¼ cups

Red Sauce

3/4 cup catsup
1/4 cup bottled chili sauce
1 tablespoon prepared
   horseradish
2 or 3 drops Tabasco
   sauce
1 teaspoon lemon juice
1 teaspoon
   Worcestershire sauce

In a small bowl combine all ingredients and mix well. Cover and refrigerate several hours to blend flavors before serving.

Makes about 1 cup

The Meat Market

Meat is still the popular choice for many entrées. It is a good source of protein, vitamins, and minerals and is full of hearty flavor. Due to consumer demands, breeding methods have been improved resulting in the production of leaner cuts and better quality. This is especially true of pork.

Meat Basics

- Buy well-trimmed beef with a small amount of marbling (fat). It should be bright red in color. Pork should be fine grained and grayish in color. Ham should be firm, pink in color, and fine grained. Lamb should be pinkish red with a velvety texture.

- Allow ¼ to ⅓ pound of meat per serving for lean, boneless cuts, ½ pound per serving for cuts with a medium amount of bone, and 1 pound per serving for very heavily boned cuts, such as ribs.

- Refrigerate meat immediately after purchase. Packaged meat may be stored in the refrigerator for 2 to 3 days or rewrapped in heavy aluminum foil or freezer wrap and frozen. Hamburger can be frozen for 2 or 3 months, other cuts for 6 to 12 months. Label all packages with contents and date. Always thaw meat in the refrigerator, not at room temperature. Use thawed meat immediately. Do not refreeze completely thawed meat.

- Wash all work surfaces, utensils, and hands thoroughly with soap and hot water after preparing raw meats to prevent cross-contamination.

- The method of cooking is determined by the cut. Tender cuts are cooked quickly with dry heat; the fibrous, less tender cuts need long, moist cooking. Beef cuts may be cooked to taste. Hamburger should, however, be well done to kill *E. coli* bacteria that may be present throughout the meat. Pork may now be cooked in less time than it previously required.

- To reduce calories and cholesterol, choose cooking methods that do not call for additional fat, such as broiling, roasting, or grilling.

Broiled New York Steak with Garlic Crumb Topping

Either New York steaks or fillets may be used for this recipe. The topping adds interest and flavor. Serve with Curried Seafood (page 22), Mesclun Salad with Feta Cheese and Walnuts with Balsamic Vinaigrette (page 55), and Scalloped Potatoes with Red Pepper (page 178). Chocolate Fudge Pie with Hazelnut Whipped Cream (page 265) makes a good company dessert.

TOPPING
1/4 cup butter or
    margarine
2 cloves garlic, minced
3/4 cup dry bread crumbs,
    preferably sourdough
1 tablespoon Dijon
    mustard
Salt and freshly ground
    pepper to taste

4 New York steaks,
    6 ounces each

In a small skillet over medium heat melt butter. Add garlic and sauté 1 minute. Add remaining ingredients, and stir until well mixed, about 1 minute. Set aside.

Preheat broiler. Place steaks on broiler pan 1½ to 2 inches from heat, and broil about 6 minutes on 1 side. Turn and broil 5 minutes on the other side. Season with salt and pepper. Divide topping equally among steaks and broil until crumbs are golden and steak is slightly pink on the inside for medium, about 1 to 2 minutes longer. Serve immediately.

Flank Steak Stuffed with Mushrooms

The mushroom-onion stuffing makes this flank steak special for company. Garden Salad (page 52) with Sevé French Dressing (page 53), Orzo with Parmesan Cheese (page 202), Steamed Carrots and Zucchini Strips (page 170), and Fresh Peach Crisp (page 257) complete this menu.

1 flank steak, about 2 pounds

2 tablespoons butter or margarine

1/2 cup chopped yellow onion

2 cloves garlic, minced

1/2 pound small mushrooms, sliced

1 tablespoon lemon juice

1/2 teaspoon salt

1/4 teaspoon marjoram, crumbled

1/4 teaspoon thyme, crumbled

1 teaspoon Dijon mustard

1/4 cup red wine

With a sharp knife and starting at the edge of the steak, cut a pocket lengthwise into the center of the steak. Place meat on a broiler pan.

In a small skillet melt butter over medium heat and sauté onion and garlic until slightly soft, about 2 minutes. Add mushrooms and sauté until vegetables are tender, about 5 minutes longer. Add lemon juice, seasonings, mustard, and 2 tablespoons wine, and mix well. Fill the pocket of the steak with the mushroom-onion mixture.

Preheat broiler. Baste top of steak with remaining wine. Broil about 6 minutes. Turn carefully and baste with wine. Broil 5 to 6 minutes longer for medium rare (do not overcook). Transfer to a cutting board or platter and let stand 5 minutes. Slice diagonally across the grain and serve immediately.

Rolled Beef Roast with Onion Sauce

For a special company dinner, serve Crab-Filled Mushrooms (page 17), Caesar Salad San Francisco Style (page 50), Whipped Potatoes with Horseradish (page 179), Steamed Broccoli and Cauliflower with Walnuts (page 164), and Hazelnut Cheesecake (page 268).

1 rolled sirloin tip roast, about 4 pounds
Onion Sauce (recipe follows)
3 cloves garlic, sliced
Salt and freshly ground pepper to taste

Remove roast from refrigerator 30 minutes before cooking and prepare Onion Sauce.

Preheat oven to 450°F. Using the tip of a sharp knife, make slits in meat. Insert garlic slices into slits. Season with salt and pepper on all sides. Place roast on rack in a shallow roasting pan.

Roast until well browned, about 15 minutes. Reduce oven temperature to 350°F. Spoon about 3 tablespoons Onion Sauce over meat. Roast, 25 minutes to the pound or until meat thermometer registers 145° to 150°F for medium rare, about 2½ hours. Baste with Onion Sauce several times during cooking.

Remove from oven and let stand 10 to 15 minutes before carving. Arrange slices on a warmed platter and pour any remaining Onion Sauce over top. Serve.

Onion Sauce

⅓ cup butter or
    margarine
1 cup chopped yellow
    onion
¾ cup dry white wine
2 tablespoons chopped
    fresh parsley
½ teaspoon salt

In a skillet over medium heat, melt
butter. Add onion and sauté until soft,
about 5 minutes. Add wine, parsley,
and salt, and simmer 1 minute longer.
Remove from heat and use for
basting beef.

Makes about 1¼ cups

Prime Rib with Baked Mushroom Caps and Horseradish Sauce

Serve this top-of-the-line beef roast for a special celebration. Start with Broiled Shrimp Rounds (page 14) and Garden Salad (page 52). Accompany the beef with Whipped Potatoes with Carrots and Garlic (page 134) and Tomato-Broccoli Cups (page 165). Serve Sour Cream Lemon Pie (page 264) for a satisfying ending.

6 pounds beef rib roast
4 cloves garlic, minced
1 teaspoon salt
1/2 teaspoon freshly
  ground pepper
Baked Mushroom Caps
  (recipe follows)
Horseradish Sauce (recipe
  follows)

Salt and freshly ground
  pepper to taste
Parsley sprigs, for garnish

One hour before roasting remove beef from refrigerator.

Preheat oven to 450°F. In a small bowl make a paste of garlic, salt, and pepper and rub on all surfaces of meat. Place meat fat-side up in a shallow roasting pan. Roast 30 minutes, reduce temperature to 325°F. Do not add water or cover.

Roast, uncovered, to desired doneness, about 20 minutes per pound, or when meat thermometer inserted in the center and not touching bones reaches 145° to 150°F for medium rare; about 2 hours longer.

Turn oven to 350°F, and transfer meat to a carving board or platter. Cover loosely with foil and let stand 15 minutes before carving.

To make beef sauce (if desired), skim off fat from juices in roasting pan. Place pan over medium-high heat and add liquid from mushrooms. Bring to a boil, scraping up pan drippings. Reduce heat and simmer until slightly reduced, about 5 minutes. Season with salt and pepper. Strain, and pass in a bowl with the roast.

Carve roast and arrange on a warmed platter and garnish with mushrooms. Tuck in parsley sprigs. Serve with Horseradish Sauce.

Baked Mushroom Caps

1 pound large mushrooms
    of equal size (about 16)
1/4 cup dry red wine
1 cup beef broth
1/4 teaspoon dried thyme,
    crumbled
1 tablespoon butter or
    margarine
Horseradish Sauce (recipe
    follows)

While meat is resting, slice stems off mushrooms. Arrange caps in an 8- by 8-inch lightly oiled or sprayed baking dish. In a small bowl mix wine, broth, and thyme together and pour over mushrooms. Dot each mushroom with a small piece of butter. Bake mushrooms, uncovered, 20 minutes. Baste with broth mixture once while baking.

Horseradish Sauce

1 tablespoon peeled and
    grated fresh
    horseradish, or 1 to 2
    tablespoons prepared
    horseradish (to taste)
1/2 cup light sour cream
1/4 cup plain nonfat yogurt
1/4 teaspoon dry mustard

In a bowl combine all ingredients. Cover and refrigerate. Serve at room temperature in a bowl.

Makes about 3/4 cup

Dijon Beef Tenderloin

Great for company, this simple preparation is about as quick and easy as it gets. Serve with Hot Shrimp Hors d'Oeuvre (page 16), Spinach, Pear, and Walnut Salad with Raspberry Vinaigrette (page 48), Baked Potato Strips with Cheese (page 175), and Apricot and Blueberry Flan (page 267).

1 beef tenderloin (about 2 to 2½ pounds)
1 clove garlic, sliced
Dijon mustard
Salt and freshly ground pepper to taste

Preheat oven to 350°F. With a sharp knife make several slits in meat and insert garlic slices. Spread lightly with mustard and season with salt and pepper.

Bake until meat thermometer registers 145° to 150°F, about 1¼ hours, for medium rare. Let stand 10 minutes before carving.

Slow-baked Barbecued Beef Roast

SERVES **6** TO **8**

Fork-tender beef, baked in a spicy baste, makes wonderful sandwiches for a light supper. Serve with an assorted fruit plate.

BEEF BASTE
3 tablespoons flour
1 tablespoon packed
   brown sugar
1/2 teaspoon salt
1/2 teaspoon dry mustard
1/2 cup catsup
1 tablespoon Worcester-
   shire sauce
1 tablespoon red wine
   vinegar
2 cloves garlic, minced
2 drops Tabasco sauce

2 1/2 to 3 pounds bottom
   or top round, 1 to 1 1/2
   inches thick (flat cut)
Kaiser rolls or hamburger
   buns

Preheat oven to 300°F. In a small bowl stir baste ingredients together. Spread half the baste in the middle of a large piece of heavy duty foil. Place meat on top of sauce and spread remaining baste over meat. Fold up foil and seal tightly. Place on a baking sheet with a rim. Bake until very tender, 5 to 6 hours.

To serve, place chunks of meat on heated rolls.

Beef Brisket

Brisket is a cut of beef taken from the breast section. This is a flat cut with minimal fat and requires long, slow cooking. Corned beef is made from this cut, but it is loaded with sodium and additives. For a special St. Patrick's Day Dinner, serve the brisket with Super Spuds with Toppings (page 176), Irish Soda Bread (recipe follows), Braised Cabbage with Apples (page 167), and Fruit Trifle (page 272) for dessert.

4 to 5 pounds beef brisket, flat cut
2 tablespoons soy sauce
2 tablespoons red wine vinegar
2 cloves garlic, minced
2 teaspoons Worcester-shire sauce
1 cup beef broth
1 tablespoon prepared mustard
1 tablespoon prepared horseradish sauce
Freshly ground pepper to taste
1 yellow onion, sliced
Spicy Mustard Sauce (recipe follows)

Remove excess fat from brisket and place in a nonaluminum baking pan. In a bowl combine remaining ingredients, except onion, and pour over brisket. Cover and marinate 4 to 5 hours or overnight in refrigerator, turning once.

Remove brisket from refrigerator 1 hour before roasting. Preheat oven to 350°F. Roast in marinade, covered, for 2 hours, basting several times. Place onion rings on top of brisket and baste again. Roast, covered, until meat is tender, about 1 hour longer. Remove brisket from pan and let stand 10 minutes before carving. Slice brisket thinly across the grain and serve immediately. Pass the Spicy Mustard Sauce.

Spicy Mustard Sauce

1 tablespoon brown
  sugar
1 teaspoon cider vinegar
1/2 teaspoon dill weed
1/4 cup Dijon mustard
1/4 cup prepared mustard
2 teaspoons vegetable oil

In a small bowl stir together the sugar with the vinegar until sugar is dissolved. Stir in remaining ingredients and mix well. Cover and chill. Serve at room temperature.

Makes about 1/2 cup

Irish Soda Bread

This classic peasant bread is one of the specialties of Ireland and is still baked in countless farm houses and homes all over the country. It is best served fresh or as toast the next day.

2 cups all-purpose flour
1 1/2 teaspoons baking
  powder
1 teaspoon salt
1/4 teaspoon baking soda
1 cup buttermilk
Butter or margarine, for
  greasing baking sheet

Preheat oven to 350°F. In a large bowl mix flour, baking powder, salt, and baking soda. Stir buttermilk into flour mixture until the dough is moistened evenly. On a floured surface knead dough 5 or 6 times. Form dough into a ball. Transfer to a buttered baking sheet and shape into a mound. With a sharp knife cut a shallow cross in the top. Bake until golden brown, about 40 minutes. Remove from pan, wrap in a clean kitchen towel, and cool on a rack for 1 hour. Break into pieces to serve.

Serves 4 to 6

Bloody Mary Beef Roast

This less-tender cut of beef cooked in a flavorful sauce makes a good informal dinner. Serve with noodles and a mixed green salad with Creamy Mayonnaise Dressing (page 65).

3 1/2 to 4 pounds boneless bottom round roast
2 or 3 cloves garlic, sliced
Salt and freshly ground pepper to taste
1 cup spicy vegetable juice or tomato juice
1 tablespoon prepared horseradish
1 clove garlic, minced
1 tablespoon prepared mustard
1 tablespoon vodka or white wine vinegar
1 teaspoon Worcestershire sauce
Celery stalks, for garnish
Gravy (recipe follows)

Preheat oven to 400°F. Place roast in a roasting pan. Make slits in roast with the tip of a sharp knife and insert garlic slices into meat. Season with salt and pepper. Roast, uncovered, for 15 minutes.

Meanwhile, in a cup stir together juice, horseradish, garlic, mustard, and Worcestershire sauce. Pour sauce over meat. Reduce heat to 350°F and bake, covered, 2 1/2 hours. Baste with sauce several times while roasting.

Remove meat to a platter and let stand 10 minutes before carving. Make gravy, if desired. Serve beef slices on a platter and garnish with celery stalks. Pass the gravy.

Variation: Vegetables (carrots, turnip, potato, onion, etc.) may be added in the last hour of cooking time.

Gravy

1 tablespoon cornstarch
1/4 cup water

In a cup blend cornstarch and water. Place roasting pan containing liquid and juices from meat over high heat. Stir in cornstarch mixture and bring to a boil stirring constantly until thickened, about 2 minutes. Serve with meat.

Makes about 1 cup

Beer Beef Stew and Parslied Dumplings

This warming stew with old-fashioned dumplings is a favorite with everyone. Serve it with a tossed green salad with Homemade Ranch Dressing (page 53), Honey-Butter Carrots (page 168), and plenty of warm crusty bread.

¼ to ⅓ cup flour

¼ teaspoon salt

¼ teaspoon freshly ground pepper

3 pounds lean stew meat, cut into 1-inch cubes

¼ to ⅓ cup vegetable oil

2 yellow onions, sliced and rings separated

6 cloves garlic, minced

2 cups beef broth, regular strength

1 cup beer, allowed to go flat

1 bay leaf

1 tablespoon brown sugar

2 tablespoons red wine vinegar

1 tablespoon Dijon mustard

2 teaspoons dried thyme, crumbled

½ cup chopped parsley

2 teaspoons salt

¼ teaspoon freshly ground pepper

Parslied Dumplings (recipe follows)

Preheat oven to 350°F. On a piece of waxed paper mix flour, salt, and pepper. Dredge meat in mixture. In a large skillet on medium-high heat warm 2 tablespoons oil. Brown meat in batches, adding more oil as needed. With a slotted spoon remove meat to a lightly oiled or sprayed 4-quart casserole. Add 1 tablespoon oil to skillet and sauté onion and garlic until soft, about 5 minutes. Add to meat in casserole. Add broth and beer to skillet and stir with a wooden spoon to loosen browned bits. Add remaining ingredients to broth and bring to a boil. Pour over meat and onions in casserole. Bake, covered, until meat is tender, 1½ to 2 hours.

Make dumplings. Remove casserole from oven. Remove bay leaf and discard. Drop dumpling batter by heaping tablespoonfuls on top of casserole. Return to oven and bake, uncovered, until dumplings are firm, 10 to 12 minutes. Serve meat and dumplings in the casserole.

Parslied Dumplings

1 cup all-purpose flour
2 teaspoons baking
  powder
1/4 teaspoon salt
1/8 teaspoon white pepper
2 tablespoons vegetable
  shortening
1/4 cup chopped parsley
1/2 cup milk

In a bowl combine flour, baking powder, salt, and pepper. With a pastry blender cut in shortening until mixture looks like coarse crumbs. Stir in parsley. Stir in milk until just combined.

Makes about 12 dumplings

Glazed Meat Loaf

Loaded with extras and topped with a flavorful glaze, this meat loaf is terrific. Use only top-quality lean ground beef. Serve with a tossed green salad, baked potatoes, corn, and Frosted Chocolate Cookies (page 283) for a family dinner. Leftovers make great sandwiches the next day.

1¼ pounds lean ground beef

¼ pound bulk pork sausage

½ cup dried bread crumbs

1 egg

1 cup chopped mushrooms

½ cup chopped yellow onion

¼ cup chopped parsley

½ cup chopped green or red bell pepper

2 cloves garlic, minced

½ cup milk

½ teaspoon dried thyme, crumbled

¾ teaspoon salt

Freshly grated pepper to taste

Meat Loaf Glaze (recipe follows)

Preheat oven to 350°F. In a large bowl mix all ingredients except glaze thoroughly. Turn into a lightly oiled or sprayed 9- by 5-inch loaf pan. Bake 30 minutes.

Remove from oven and pour off any grease that may have accumulated. Spread with glaze. Return to oven and bake until meat is no longer pink, about 35 minutes longer. Let stand 10 minutes in the pan. Remove from pan, slice, and serve immediately.

Meat Loaf Glaze

1 tablespoon brown
   sugar
1 tablespoon cider
   vinegar
¼ cup catsup
2 teaspoons Dijon
   mustard

In a small bowl dissolve sugar in vinegar.
Whisk in catsup and mustard.

Makes ⅓ cup

Coffee Beef Stew

Browning the meat and adding coffee makes a rich flavorful sauce for this long-simmering stew. Fresh beans, warm sourdough bread, and Blueberry Pie (page 260) for dessert complete the meal.

¼ cup flour

¾ teaspoon salt

Freshly ground pepper to taste

1½ pounds stew meat or round steak, cut into bite-sized pieces

1 to 2 tablespoons vegetable oil

1 cup coffee

1 can (8 ounces) tomato sauce

1 tablespoon red wine vinegar

2 teaspoons caraway seed

3 to 4 carrots, sliced into 1-inch pieces

1 yellow onion, quartered

6 very small new potatoes, unpeeled

Preheat oven to 350°F. On a piece of waxed paper mix flour, salt, and pepper. Dredge meat in flour mixture. In a large skillet brown meat in 1 tablespoon oil on medium-high heat until well browned, 8 to 10 minutes. Add more oil as needed.

Add coffee, tomato sauce, red wine vinegar, and any flour left over from dredging. Stir in caraway seeds and bring to a boil.

Place vegetables in a 3- to 4-quart lightly oiled or sprayed casserole. Pour meat mixture over vegetables. Bake, covered, 1½ hours.

Chile Meatballs

These meatballs with chiles are browned in the oven so browning in oil is not necessary. They are then baked again in a tangy sauce. Serve with Romaine-Bacon-Apple Salad (page 56) and Baked Polenta (page 215).

1½ pounds lean
    hamburger
½ cup fine bread crumbs
1 egg
¼ cup red wine
½ teaspoon dried
    oregano, crumbled
¾ teaspoon salt
¼ teaspoon freshly
    ground pepper
1 can (4 ounces) diced
    chiles, drained
Tangy Beer-Tomato Sauce
    (page 9)

Preheat oven to 400°F. In a bowl combine all ingredients except sauce. Shape into 1-inch balls. Place on a rimmed cookie sheet and bake 10 minutes. Discard any grease that may have accumulated. Transfer to an oiled 2-quart casserole.

Reduce oven temperature to 350°F. Pour sauce over meatballs and bake, covered, until sauce is bubbly and meatballs are warmed through, about 35 minutes.

Chili with Toppings

Serve this flavorful chili with assorted toppings for a casual get-together after a football game or for game watching at home. Offer Chunky Guacamole (page 24) with tortilla chips, pretzels, and raw vegetables for snacking and Cheese Bread (recipe follows) to go with the chili. These recipes can be doubled for a crowd.

1 pound lean ground beef

1 cup chopped yellow onion

1 can (14½ ounces) whole tomatoes including juices, chopped

1 can (16 ounces) tomato sauce

1 tablespoon chili powder, plus more to taste if desired

1 teaspoon salt

¼ teaspoon paprika

¼ teaspoon cinnamon

¼ teaspoon ground cumin

¼ teaspoon allspice

1 tablespoon cocoa powder

¼ teaspoon ground cloves

2 cans (16 ounces each) dark red kidney beans, partially drained

TOPPINGS

Grated Cheddar cheese

Plain nonfat yogurt or sour cream

Chopped green onions including some tender green tops

In a large saucepan over medium heat, cook meat with onion until meat is browned and onion is soft, stirring occasionally about 10 minutes.

Add tomatoes, tomato sauce, and seasonings and mix well. Simmer, covered, 10 minutes.

Stir in beans and simmer, uncovered, until flavors are blended, about 20 minutes longer. Ladle into bowls and pass the toppings.

Cheese Bread

1 loaf sourdough French bread, split lengthwise

1 cup grated Monterey Jack cheese

1 cup grated Cheddar cheese

3 tablespoons freshly grated Parmesan cheese

Preheat oven to 350°F. Slice bread into 1-inch slices. Place on a baking sheet and sprinkle with cheeses. Bake until cheese is bubbly, about 10 minutes.

Makes about 24 pieces

Party Spaghetti and Meatballs

This spicy sauce with a lot of meatballs makes a perfect dish to serve for a crowd. Start the party with an Antipasto Platter (page 4) with wine, beer, or soft drinks. The antipasto can serve as the salad, or add a mixed green salad with Italian Dressing (page 56), warm garlic bread, and assorted cookies for dessert.

SPICY SPAGHETTI SAUCE

- 1 can (46 ounces) tomato juice
- 1 can (6 ounces) tomato paste
- 1 can (15 ounces) tomato purée
- 1 cup beef broth
- 1/2 teaspoon celery seed
- 1/4 teaspoon dry mustard
- 1/2 teaspoon dried basil, crumbled
- 1/4 teaspoon oregano, crumbled
- 1/2 teaspoon chili powder
- 1/4 teaspoon salt
- 1/4 teaspoon freshly ground pepper
- 1/2 teaspoon sugar
- 1/4 teaspoon Worcester-shire sauce
- 1 tablespoon olive oil (optional, for flavor)
- 3 cloves garlic, minced
- 1 small yellow onion, chopped
- 1/4 cup parsley, chopped

In a large saucepan combine all the sauce ingredients and bring to a boil. Reduce heat to low and simmer, uncovered, 10 minutes. Remove pickling spice bag and discard. Cover and simmer slowly 1 hour.

While sauce is cooking, make meatballs. Add meatballs to sauce and simmer, uncovered, until flavors are blended and sauce is slightly thickened, 30 minutes longer. Serve on spaghetti and sprinkle with Parmesan cheese.

½ cup chopped
  mushrooms
1 tablespoon mixed
  pickling spices, placed
  in a cheesecloth bag
  or tea infuser

Meatballs (recipe follows)
16 ounces spaghetti,
  cooked
Freshly grated Parmesan
  Cheese, for topping

Meatballs

2 pounds lean ground
  beef
¼ cup finely chopped
  yellow onion
¼ teaspoon ground
  allspice
1 tablespoon freshly
  grated Parmesan
  cheese
½ teaspoon poultry
  seasonings
½ cup flour
½ cup milk
¼ teaspoon salt
Freshly ground pepper
  to taste

In a large bowl mix all ingredients
together. Cover and refrigerate 1 hour
(for easier handling).

Preheat oven to 400°F. Form mixture
into 1-inch balls and place on a baking
sheet. Bake until browned, about 15
minutes. Remove from pan and discard
any grease.

Makes about 50 meatballs

Rack of Lamb

This makes an elegant presentation for a company dinner. If desired, have the butcher "French" the bones (strip the upper bone of the meat). These can be dressed after cooking with paper collars, but it is not necessary. For easy serving, have the chops cracked at the base. For an hors d'oeuvre, serve Sun-dried Tomato and Feta Cheese Dip (page 21). Accompany the lamb with Greek Salad with Feta Cheese (page 49), Basmati Rice with Nuts and Spices (page 209), Tzatziki (recipe follows) or mint jelly, and a green vegetable. Serve Toffee Nut Bars (page 284) for dessert.

2 tablespoons Dijon mustard

2 teaspoons chopped fresh rosemary, or 1 teaspoon dried rosemary, crumbled

2 cloves garlic, minced

1 teaspoon salt

1 rack of lamb (24 ribs, about 4½ to 5 pounds)

Freshly ground pepper to taste

Mint leaves, for garnish

Tzatziki (recipe follows)

Mint jelly, purchased (optional)

Preheat oven to 400°F. In a small bowl mix mustard, rosemary, garlic, and salt. Spread the fat side of the rack with the mustard mixture. Sprinkle with pepper. Place rack on shallow roasting pan with fat side up and roast until medium, about 35 to 40 minutes.

Slice chops apart and transfer to a platter. Garnish with mint leaves and serve with Tzatziki or mint jelly.

Tzatziki (Greek Cucumber–Yogurt Dip)

A Greek-inspired cucumber and yogurt dip or sauce to serve with Pocket Bread Wedges (page 25) as an appetizer or as a sauce with lamb or seafood. Drain yogurt several hours before using.

1 cucumber, peeled, halved, seeded, and grated

1 cup plain nonfat yogurt, drained (see note)

1 large clove garlic, minced

1 teaspoon lemon juice

1 tablespoon minced fresh mint leaves, or 1 tablespoon chopped parsley

Salt and freshly ground pepper to taste

Place grated cucumber between paper towels for 20 minutes to absorb extra moisture, then pat dry.

In a bowl combine drained yogurt and cucumber with remaining ingredients and mix well. Cover and refrigerate. Serve at room temperature.

Makes about 2 cups

Note: To drain yogurt, place in a sieve lined with a coffee filter over a deep bowl in the refrigerator for several hours or overnight.

Broiled Lamb Chops with Dijon–Mayonnaise Topping

SERVES 4

Lamb seems to suggest a spring dinner, however it is generally available all year round. Serve with Couscous with Pine Nuts (page 205), Minted Carrots (page 169) garnished with mint leaves, and Citrus-Nut Cake (page 276) for dessert.

DIJON-MAYONNAISE TOPPING

1/3 cup light mayonnaise

2 teaspoons Dijon mustard

1 tablespoon finely chopped fresh rosemary, or 1/2 teaspoon dried rosemary, crumbled

1 clove garlic, minced

1/4 teaspoon salt

Freshly ground pepper to taste

8 lamb chops, 1 to 1 1/4 inches thick

Preheat broiler. To make topping, in a small bowl stir together mayonnaise, mustard, rosemary, garlic, salt, and pepper.

Place lamb chops on broiler pan 3 to 4 inches from heat. Broil 5 minutes. Turn chops over and broil 4 minutes longer. Spread mayonnaise mixture evenly on top of chops and broil until chops are done and topping is golden, about 4 minutes longer. Watch carefully. Serve immediately.

Pork Chops in Sour Cream Sauce

This is an easy way to prepare pork chops with a creamy sauce lightly flavored with sage. They make a nice company dinner when served with Smoked Salmon Spread (page 19), a tossed green salad, fresh asparagus, Sweet Onion and Rice Bake (page 182), and Spiced Apple Crisp (page 258).

4 large pork chops

Sage, for sprinkling on top

Salt and freshly ground pepper to taste

1 tablespoon vegetable oil

1/2 yellow onion, sliced and separated into rings

1/2 cup light sour cream

1 teaspoon Dijon mustard

1 tablespoon flour

1/2 cups chicken broth

1/4 cup dry white wine

1/4 cup chopped parsley

Preheat oven to 350°F. Sprinkle chops generously with sage. Season with salt and pepper. In a large, nonstick skillet over medium heat, warm oil. Add pork chops and brown about 5 minutes on each side. Transfer chops to a lightly oiled or sprayed 8- by 8-inch baking dish. Lay onion rings on top.

In a small bowl blend sour cream, mustard, and flour. Add broth and wine to the skillet and boil 1 minute. Whisk in sour cream mixture and parsley and blend well. Pour over chops. Bake, uncovered, until bubbly, about 35 minutes.

Herbed Pork Loin with Roasted Potatoes

Today pork is leaner and juicier and can be safely cooked to medium doneness with a little pink showing. Begin this elegant company dinner with Warm Brie and Marinated Roasted Red Peppers and Roasted Garlic (page 9) and baguette slices. Serve Spinach, Pear, and Walnut Salad with Raspberry Vinaigrette (page 48), and Cran-Applesauce (recipe follows) with the roast. Filled Pumpkin Dessert (page 271) makes a great ending, especially around Halloween.

HERB RUB
1 1/2 to 2 tablespoons vegetable oil
2 cloves garlic, minced
1 teaspoon dried thyme, crumbled
1/2 teaspoon dried rosemary, crumbled
1/2 teaspoon dried oregano, crumbled
2 tablespoons chopped parsley
1 teaspoon salt
1/4 teaspoon freshly ground pepper

1 whole, rolled pork loin roast (about 2 1/2 pounds)
4 red-skinned new potatoes, quartered
Cran-Applesauce (recipe follows)
Parsley sprigs, for garnish

Preheat oven to 350°F. In a small bowl combine herb rub ingredients and mix well. Place roast in a roasting pan. Spread herb mixture on top and on all sides of roast, leaving about 1/2 tablespoon in bowl. Add potatoes to bowl and toss with remaining mixture. Bake meat, uncovered, 1 hour.

Add potatoes to pan and bake until meat thermometer registers 160°F and potatoes are tender, 30 to 40 minutes longer. Let roast stand 10 minutes before carving. Transfer to a platter and surround with potatoes and parsley.

Cran-Applesauce

This vivid, ruby red sauce is as good as it looks. It is a wonderful side dish to serve for a holiday dinner.

3/4 cup water

1/4 cup red wine (or water)

1 cup sugar

1 package (12 ounces) cranberries, rinsed and sorted (see note)

3 Red Delicious apples (about 1 1/2 pounds), peeled, cored, and sliced

1 teaspoon lemon juice

1/4 teaspoon cinnamon

In a saucepan over medium-high heat place water, wine, and sugar, and stir to dissolve. Add cranberries, apples, and lemon juice and bring to a boil. Reduce heat and gently boil, uncovered, stirring occasionally until cranberries pop and apples are soft, about 15 minutes.

Transfer mixture to food processor and purée. Add cinnamon and mix well. Let stand several hours before serving or store, covered, in refrigerator for several days. (It will thicken as it stands.)

Makes 4 cups

Note: You can make this recipe at any time of the year using frozen cranberries.

Company Pork Chops

These thick, stuffed pork chops served with Whipped Potatoes and Carrots (page 179), a mixed green salad with Homemade Ranch Dressing (page 53), and Fruit Trifle (page 272) make a terrific company dinner.

4 pork chops, about
   1 inch thick
Salt and freshly ground
   pepper
4 slices prosciutto
4 slices Gruyère cheese
1 tablespoon vegetable oil
1 tablespoon butter or
   margarine
1/2 cup chicken broth
1/2 cup dry white wine

With a sharp knife cut into the meaty side of each chop to make a pocket. Season pockets with salt and pepper. Roll up together 1 slice each of prosciutto and cheese and flatten, then insert into pocket of chop.

In a large skillet over medium heat, brown chops in oil and butter about 4 minutes on each side. Add broth and wine, cover, and simmer 10 minutes. Turn and simmer, covered, 10 minutes longer.

Remove chops to a serving platter. Reduce liquid by boiling 5 minutes, scraping up browned bits. Return chops to pan and reheat on low heat, uncovered, about 5 minutes.
Serve immediately.

Mexican Pork Roast

Marinate this roast for eight hours or overnight in this spicy marinade for maximum flavor. Shrimp Salsa (page 15) with chips makes a nice introduction to this meal. Serve the roast with Thick Tomato Slices with Avocado Dressing (page 58), Corn and Black Bean Polenta (page 216), and follow with Flan (Crème Caramel) (page 266) for dessert.

1 pork loin, 3 to 4 pounds

MEXICAN-STYLE MARINADE
1/2 cup beer, allowed to go flat
Juice of 1 large lime
1 tablespoon vegetable oil
2 cloves garlic, minced
1/2 teaspoon thyme, crumbled
1/2 teaspoon oregano, crumbled
1/4 teaspoon ground coriander
1/4 teaspoon cumin
1 teaspoon Worcestershire sauce
Freshly ground pepper to taste

Avocado slices, for garnish
Orange slices, for garnish
Cilantro sprigs, for garnish

Place pork loin in a shallow glass dish. In a small bowl stir together all ingredients for marinade. Pour over pork. Cover and marinate 8 hours in the refrigerator, turning several times. Remove from refrigerator 1 hour before cooking.

Preheat oven to 325°F. Remove pork from marinade, reserving marinade. Place in a shallow roasting pan. Roast until meat thermometer reaches 160° to 170°F, about 1 3/4 hours. Brush with remaining marinade several times while cooking. Let stand 10 minutes before carving. Add garnishes and serve immediately.

The Vegetable Stand

In many menus, vegetables often take center stage and become the main part of the meal. Creative recipes make vegetables exciting to prepare and inviting to eat. Improved growing methods and air transportation have extended the season and availability of most produce. Produce departments present a large selection of vegetables year around at reasonable prices. In the summer months, the choicest and most flavorful vegetables can be found at roadside stands and farmers' markets. Eating the recommended two to three vegetable servings a day should be no problem.

Vegetable Basics

Select vegetables that are firm to the touch and free from soft spots and blemishes.

Store most vegetables in the refrigerator after purchase in plastic bags to maintain freshness. If washing vegetables, dry well before storing. Store mushrooms in a paper bag and clean just before using. Tomatoes improve in flavor if stored at room temperature.

Cook vegetables until tender crisp to preserve flavor, color, and nutrients. Steaming is an excellent way to cook vegetables.

Vegetables stand on their own and need very little seasoning. Just a twist of lemon or a sprinkling of herbs, butter, or olive oil and salt and pepper to taste is all you need.

Fresh Asparagus and Red Pepper with Wine Sauce

This dish is nice to serve for company because it can be made ahead (see note) and baked later. If possible, bake in a decorative serving dish.

4 cups water

1/4 teaspoon salt

1 1/2 to 2 pounds fresh asparagus, tough end of stalk cut off and discarded (all spears should be same length)

1 red bell pepper, seeded and cut into narrow strips

1/4 cup white wine

3 tablespoons butter or margarine, melted

Salt and freshly ground pepper to taste

Preheat oven to 400°F. In a large pan over high heat bring water and salt to a boil. Boil asparagus and bell pepper 5 minutes. Drain under cold water. Arrange asparagus in a single layer in a long baking dish or ovenproof serving dish. Arrange peppers on top.

In a small bowl mix wine and butter and pour over asparagus and bell pepper. Season with salt and pepper. Bake until heated through, about 10 minutes.

Note: If preparing the first step ahead, cover and refrigerate. Bring to room temperature before baking.

Beets in Raspberry Vinegar Sauce

Ruby red beets are simmered in a sweet-and-sour sauce for a wonderful flavor and great eye appeal.

4 to 5 medium beets (about 1½ pounds), with 1 to 2 inches of tops left on
1 tablespoon butter or margarine
1 tablespoon brown sugar
⅓ cup raspberry vinegar

In a saucepan cover beets with water. Bring to a boil over high heat, then reduce heat and simmer, covered, until tender, 35 to 45 minutes (depending on size). Drain and cool slightly, then slip skins and tops off and cut into ¼-inch slices.

In the same saucepan combine butter, sugar, and vinegar, and stir until butter melts. Add sliced beets to sauce and simmer until heated through, about 5 minutes, stirring several times to blend flavors.

Orange Broccoli

Orange juice and zest sharpen the fresh flavor of broccoli. Cook broccoli only until it is tender crisp and still bright green.

1 large bunch broccoli, about 1 pound
1 tablespoon butter or margarine
2 tablespoons fresh orange juice
½ teaspoon orange zest
¼ teaspoon salt
Freshly ground pepper to taste

Cut off all but 1½ inches of broccoli stalks and discard. Cut broccoli into serving pieces.

In a saucepan over high heat boil enough water to cover broccoli. Add broccoli, reduce heat to medium-high and cook until tender crisp, 5 to 6 minutes. Drain in a colander.

Return broccoli to pan; add butter, orange juice, zest, salt, and pepper and toss to mix until reheated, about 2 minutes. Serve immediately.

Steamed Broccoli and Cauliflower with Walnuts

The contrast in flavor and color of these two cole crops makes an attractive presentation. Sautéed walnuts add flavor and texture.

½ head cauliflower, broken into florets

½ bunch broccoli, broken into florets

2 tablespoons butter or margarine

⅓ cup coarsely chopped walnuts

2 tablespoons fresh lemon juice

Salt and freshly ground pepper to taste

Place cauliflower florets on a steamer rack over gently boiling water, cover, and steam 5 minutes. Add broccoli and steam until vegetables are tender, about 5 minutes longer.

Meanwhile, in a small skillet melt 1 tablespoon butter over medium-high heat. Add nuts and stir until golden, about 2 minutes. Stir in remaining butter and lemon juice.

Transfer vegetables to a warm bowl and mix with nut mixture. Season with salt and pepper. Serve immediately.

Tomato-Broccoli Cups

This is a colorful company side dish that can be prepared ahead and baked later. It complements a variety of meat entrées.

1 tablespoon butter or margarine

1 tablespoon vegetable oil

2 cups chopped broccoli florets

5 or 6 mushrooms, chopped

1 clove garlic, minced

1/4 teaspoon salt

Freshly ground pepper to taste

3 tomatoes, halved

Freshly grated Parmesan cheese, for topping

Preheat oven to 350°F. In a skillet over medium heat melt butter with oil. Add broccoli, mushrooms, and garlic. Sauté until vegetables are tender crisp, about 10 minutes. Season with salt and pepper and set aside.

With a sharp knife or serrated spoon, remove pulp from tomatoes, leaving a 1/4-inch shell. Drain, cut-side down, on a paper towel for 5 minutes; then place on a cookie sheet and fill with vegetable mixture. Sprinkle with Parmesan cheese. Bake until tomatoes are heated through, about 15 minutes. Serve immediately.

Lemony Green Beans

Green beans are best when they are fresh and in season. Fresh beans should be crisp and snap when broken. Cook briefly to retain the fresh flavor and firm texture.

1 pound green beans, trimmed

2 tablespoons butter or margarine

2 cloves garlic, minced

2 tablespoons fresh lemon juice

1/2 teaspoon salt

Freshly ground pepper to taste

Place beans in a saucepan and cover with water. Bring to a boil, reduce heat to medium and cook, uncovered, until tender crisp, about 6 minutes. Drain and return to pan.

Add remaining ingredients and sauté until flavors are blended, about 1 minute. Serve immediately.

Variation: Omit lemon juice and add 2 tablespoons balsamic vinegar.

Braised Cabbage with Apples

Sweet and-sour cabbage makes a great side dish for Beef Brisket (page 138) or other meat entrées.

2 to 3 tablespoons bacon drippings, or butter or margarine

1 cup chopped yellow onion

1 small head red cabbage, about 1 1/2 pounds, cored and shredded or thinly sliced

2 Red Delicious apples, unpeeled, cored, and thinly sliced

1/4 cup red wine vinegar

1/4 cup dry red wine or water

3 tablespoons firmly packed brown sugar

3/4 teaspoon salt

In a large saucepan, warm drippings or butter over medium heat. Add onion and sauté 2 minutes. Add remaining ingredients and bring to a boil, tossing and turning until well mixed. Reduce temperature and simmer, covered, over low heat until cabbage and apples are very tender, stirring occasionally, about 1 hour.

Honey–Butter Carrots

These sweet, buttery carrots will appeal to everyone, even the kids.

6 carrots (about 1 pound), cut lengthwise into 3-inch strips

2 tablespoons butter or margarine

2 tablespoons honey

Salt and freshly ground pepper to taste

2 tablespoons chopped parsley

Place carrots on steamer rack over gently boiling water, cover, and steam until tender, about 15 minutes.

In a saucepan over medium heat melt butter with honey. Add carrots, salt, and pepper and mix well. Transfer to a bowl and sprinkle with parsley. Serve immediately.

Minted Carrots

Prepare these carrots in the summer when fresh mint is in the garden. If mint is not available, fresh dill may be used for an equally delicious flavor.

6 carrots (about 1 pound), sliced
½ cup chicken broth
2 tablespoons butter or margarine
¼ teaspoon sugar
3 tablespoons chopped fresh mint, or
  1 tablespoon snipped fresh dill, or
  1 teaspoon dill weed
Salt and freshly ground pepper to taste

In a saucepan over medium heat, combine carrots and broth. Bring to a boil, reduce heat to low, and simmer, covered, until carrots are tender, 10 to 12 minutes.

Uncover and add butter, sugar, mint, salt, and pepper, and cook, uncovered, until flavors are blended and liquid is about gone, stirring occasionally, about 5 minutes. Serve immediately.

Steamed Carrots and Zucchini Strips

The combination of carrots and zucchini makes a good contrast in color and taste. Steam until tender crisp for best results.

2 carrots, peeled or scraped
2 zucchini, ends trimmed and unpeeled
2 tablespoons butter or margarine
1 tablespoon snipped fresh dill, or
  1 teaspoon dill weed
Salt and freshly ground pepper to taste

Cut carrots and zucchini into strips about 3 inches long and ¼ inch wide. Place carrots in a steamer over gently boiling water. Cover and steam 6 minutes. Add zucchini to carrots and steam until vegetables are tender, about 8 minutes longer.

In a small pan over medium heat melt butter with dill. Transfer vegetables to a warm bowl and pour dill butter over and mix well. Add salt and pepper.

Sauté of Summer Peas and Mushrooms

Crisp snap peas and shelled peas combined with fresh mushrooms make a wonderful vegetable side dish that is easy and quick to prepare.

2 tablespoons butter or margarine

8 to 10 fresh mushrooms, sliced

1½ cups (¼ pound) fresh snap peas, washed, dried, ends trimmed, and halved

1½ cups fresh shelled peas, or 1½ cups frozen peas, thawed

Salt and freshly ground pepper to taste

1 tablespoon toasted sesame seeds (page 54) (optional)

In a medium skillet, melt butter over medium heat. Sauté mushrooms and snap peas about 3 minutes. Add fresh shelled peas and cook until vegetables are tender crisp, 3 to 4 minutes longer. Season with salt and pepper. Sprinkle with sesame seeds. Serve immediately.

Roasted Vegetables

Roasting vegetables intensifies their full flavor and adds a smoky touch. Use a variety of vegetables in season.

1 eggplant (about ¾ pound), quartered and cut into ½-inch slices

1 zucchini, cut into ⅜-inch slices

2 yellow crookneck squash, cut into ⅜-inch slices

1 red onion, cut into chunks

6 whole garlic cloves, peeled

1 red bell pepper, seeded and cut into eighths

1 tablespoon chopped mixed fresh herbs (basil, oregano, and thyme), or 1 teaspoon mixed dried herbs, crumbled

2 to 3 tablespoons olive oil

½ teaspoon salt

Freshly ground pepper to taste

1 tomato, cut into eighths

2 tablespoons balsamic vinegar

¼ cup chopped parsley

Salt and freshly ground pepper to taste

Preheat oven to 425°F. Place all vegetables and herbs except tomatoes in a jelly-roll pan. Add oil, salt, and pepper and stir to coat. Bake, uncovered, 15 minutes. Add tomatoes, sprinkle with vinegar, and mix with other vegetables.

Bake until vegetables are tender crisp and slightly browned, 15 to 20 minutes longer, stirring once. Add parsley and salt and pepper to taste. Serve immediately.

Plank Potatoes with Parmesan Cheese

These crisp potato slices go well with grilled hamburgers or as a party-time hors d'oeuvre.

2 tablespoons vegetable oil
4 large baking potatoes, scrubbed but not peeled, and sliced lengthwise into 3/8-inch slices
Salt and freshly ground pepper to taste
Paprika
Freshly grated Parmesan cheese

Preheat oven to 375°F. On a baking sheet spread oil. Add potatoes in single layer and turn in oil to coat. Sprinkle with salt, pepper, and paprika. Bake until potatoes are tender crisp, about 20 minutes. Add cheese and bake until cheese melts, about 2 minutes longer. Serve immediately.

Roasted New Potatoes

Easy to make, these potatoes go with almost any entreé.

2 to 3 tablespoons
  vegetable oil

2 cloves garlic, minced

1 teaspoon salt

Freshly ground pepper to
  taste

1/2 teaspoon dried
  rosemary, crumbled

6 red new potatoes,
  unpeeled, quartered

Preheat oven to 400°F. In a large bowl mix oil, garlic, salt, pepper, and rosemary. Add potatoes and toss well to coat. Transfer to a baking sheet and bake until golden brown and crisp, stirring once, 50 to 55 minutes.

Baked Potato Strips with Cheese

The potatoes bake in the oven along with the main course for an easy oven meal.

4 new potatoes, unpeeled and cut into strips like French fries
¼ cup low-fat milk
½ teaspoon Tabasco sauce
½ teaspoon salt
Freshly ground pepper to taste
1 cup grated Cheddar cheese

Preheat oven to 350°F. Place potatoes in a bowl of water while preparing to keep them from discoloring. Drain and dry with paper towels. Place in a lightly oiled or sprayed 7½- by 11¾-inch baking dish.

In a small bowl mix milk, Tabasco, salt, and pepper; pour over potatoes and mix well. Bake, uncovered, until potatoes are tender crisp, stirring once, about 45 minutes. Sprinkle with cheese and bake until cheese is melted, about 5 minutes longer.

Super Spuds with Toppings

Arrange a bowl of baked potatoes on a table or bar and offer several assorted toppings for guests to help themselves.

1 or 2 baking potatoes
  per person
Vegetable oil for rubbing
  on potatoes
Sour Cream and Blue
  Cheese Topping (recipe
  follows)
Assorted toppings
  (suggestions follow)

ASSORTED TOPPINGS
Grated Cheddar,
  Monterey Jack, or
  Swiss cheese
Freshly grated Parmesan
  cheese
Crumbled blue cheese
Chopped mushrooms
Roasted garlic
Cottage cheese
Sour cream or plain
  nonfat yogurt
Crumbled bacon or diced
  ham
Sliced green onions
Chopped ripe olives
Diced chiles
Chopped parsley
Grated carrots
Salsa
Fresh chopped herbs with
  butter
Chopped tomatoes

Preheat oven to 375°F. Scrub potatoes thoroughly. Dry and rub lightly with oil (for a softer skin). Prick potatoes with a sharp fork in several places to allow steam to escape. Bake until tender, about 1 hour, depending on size. Cut a criss-cross in the top of each potato and press the ends in and up. Add desired toppings.

Sour Cream and Blue Cheese Topping

½ cup light sour cream

½ cup plain nonfat yogurt

2 tablespoons crumbled blue cheese

2 tablespoons chopped parsley

2 tablespoons chopped green onion

In a small bowl combine all ingredients.

Makes enough for 6 potatoes

Scalloped Potatoes with Red Pepper

Red pepper and parsley add color and a new flavor to an old-fashioned dish. For a speedy preparation, use the food processor for slicing the potatoes.

4 large potatoes (about 2 pounds), peeled and sliced

1 small yellow onion, thinly sliced

1 red bell pepper, seeded and chopped

1/3 cup chopped parsley

1 cup milk

2 tablespoons flour

1 teaspoon salt

Freshly ground pepper to taste

1 teaspoon paprika

1/2 teaspoon dry mustard

1 cup grated Cheddar cheese

Preheat oven to 350°F. In a 2-quart lightly oiled or sprayed casserole, layer half the potatoes, then all the onion, bell pepper, and parsley. Top with remaining potatoes. In a small bowl whisk together milk, flour, salt, pepper, paprika, and dry mustard. Pour over potatoes. Do not stir. Cover and bake until potatoes are tender, about 1 hour. Sprinkle with cheese and bake, uncovered, until cheese is melted, about 10 minutes longer. Serve immediately.

Whipped Potatoes with Carrots and Garlic

SERVES 6

Whipped (mashed) potatoes are making a comeback but with variations. This version includes flecks of orange and green and is lightly flavored with garlic.

7 to 8 russet baking potatoes (about 2½ pounds), peeled and halved lengthwise

2 carrots, sliced

4 to 6 cloves garlic, peeled

¼ teaspoon salt, for cooking water

½ to ¾ cup buttermilk or milk

1 to 2 tablespoons butter or margarine

½ teaspoon salt

Freshly ground pepper to taste

3 tablespoons chopped parsley

In a large saucepan place potatoes, carrots, and garlic. Cover with enough water to clear vegetables by ½ inch. Bring to a boil over high heat, reduce to low, cover, and cook until vegetables are soft, about 20 minutes. Drain thoroughly. Add ½ to ¾ cup buttermilk and beat vegetables with an electric mixer. Use additional milk if needed to make them light and fluffy. Beat in butter in small pieces. Add salt, pepper, and parsley and fluff with a fork. Transfer to a warmed bowl and serve immediately.

Variation: For whipped potatoes with horseradish, omit carrots and garlic and add 2 tablespoons prepared horseradish.

Potato Pancakes

A traditional German side dish to accompany Beef Brisket (page 138). Serve with applesauce and light sour cream.

5 to 6 raw potatoes (about 2 pounds), peeled and grated
1/2 yellow onion, finely chopped
2 eggs, beaten
2 tablespoons flour
1/2 teaspoon salt
1/8 teaspoon white pepper
3 tablespoons vegetable oil, for frying

In a food processor grate potatoes. Place in a bowl of salted water to prevent their discoloring. When ready to use, drain and pat with paper towels to remove excess moisture. In a bowl combine potatoes with remaining ingredients except oil. On a plate divide into 6 or 8 mounds (about 1/2 cup each).

In a 12-inch, nonstick skillet over medium-high heat, heat oil. Place potatoes in pan with hot oil and flatten with a spatula. Cook until golden brown and crisp, 5 to 6 minutes on each side. Remove with a spatula and drain on a paper towel. (You may have to do this in batches.) Keep warm in a 300°F oven, up to 15 minutes.

New Potato and Blue Cheese Pie

This combination of new potatoes and blue cheese makes a complementary side dish for beef. As the blue cheese melts with the broth it forms a delicious sauce coating the potato slices.

6 new potatoes (about 2 pounds), unpeeled and sliced

Salt and freshly ground pepper to taste

1/2 cup crumbled blue cheese

1/2 cup chicken broth

Preheat oven to 350°F. In a 10- by 2-inch lightly oiled or sprayed deep-dish pie plate, arrange half of the potato slices. Season with salt and pepper. Sprinkle blue cheese evenly over potatoes. Add remaining potato slices and season with salt and pepper again. Pour broth around the edge.

Cover tightly with foil and bake until potatoes are tender, about 35 minutes. Remove foil and cook until potatoes are lightly browned, about 10 minutes longer.

Sweet Onion and Rice Bake

This is a great dish, combining a starch and a vegetable into one casserole. It goes well with all meats. Use sweet onions such as Vidalia, Walla Walla, or Texas Sweet if available.

½ cup long-grain white rice

4 cups water

½ teaspoon salt

3 or 4 large sweet onions, sliced and separated into rings (about 8 cups) (see note)

½ cup chicken broth

1½ cups (about 8 ounces) grated Swiss cheese

¼ cup milk

¼ teaspoon salt

⅛ teaspoon white pepper

¼ cup chopped parsley

Preheat oven to 350°F. In a large pan over high heat boil rice in water and salt 5 minutes. Drain and place in a lightly oiled or sprayed 4-quart casserole. Add onions, broth, cheese, milk, salt, and pepper and mix well. Bake, covered, 1 hour, stirring once. Stir in parsley and bake, covered, until onions and rice are tender, 5 to 10 minutes longer.

Note: To slice onions easily and quickly use a food processor.

Steamed Spinach and Garlic

Spinach has a way of disappearing as it cooks. Allow at least ¾ pound per person. Steaming is a simple way to cook spinach to retain the fresh taste and bright green color. The garlic adds flavor.

1 bag (3 pounds) prewashed spinach, coarse stems removed

4 to 6 cloves garlic, peeled and thinly sliced

Butter or margarine to taste

Salt and freshly ground pepper to taste

In a large steamer pan over medium-high heat, place spinach and garlic over water. Cook, covered, until spinach is wilted, about 5 minutes, tossing several times with a fork. Transfer to a warm bowl. Season with butter, salt, and pepper. Serve immediately.

Broiled Tomato Slices

Broiled tomato slices make a nice accompaniment to almost any entrée. They serve as a vegetable and add color to the plate.

3 tomatoes, cut into
⅜-inch slices (do not
use end pieces)

Olive oil, for brushing on
tomatoes

Dried herbs (oregano,
basil, and marjoram)

Salt and freshly ground
pepper to taste

Freshly grated Parmesan
cheese

¼ cup finely chopped
parsley

Prepare broiler. Place tomato slices on broiler pan. Brush with oil and sprinkle with herbs, salt, pepper, cheese, and parsley. Broil until warmed through, about 3 minutes. Serve immediately.

Summertime Casserole

A combination of garden-fresh zucchini and vine-ripened tomatoes layered with cheese makes a delicious side dish.

1 tablespoon vegetable oil

1/2 cup chopped yellow onion

1 clove garlic, minced

3 zucchini or crookneck squash, or a combination (about 1 1/2 pounds), sliced into 3/8-inch slices

1/2 teaspoon salt

Freshly ground pepper to taste

1 tablespoon snipped fresh dill, or 1/2 teaspoon dried dill weed

3 small tomatoes, seeded and sliced

1 cup grated Cheddar cheese

1 tablespoon butter or margarine

1 cup fresh bread crumbs

2 tablespoons Parmesan cheese

Preheat oven to 350°F. In a large skillet warm oil over medium heat. Sauté onion, garlic, and zucchini, until slightly soft, about 5 minutes. Season with salt, pepper, and dill.

In a lightly oiled or sprayed 3- or 4-quart casserole layer zucchini mixture, tomatoes, and cheese in 2 layers.

In the same skillet melt butter. Add bread crumbs and toss to coat. Sprinkle crumb mixture on top of vegetables. Sprinkle with Parmesan cheese. Bake, uncovered, until vegetables are tender, 40 to 45 minutes. Serve immediately.

Vegetable and Fresh Herb Casserole

An easy side dish to serve with grilled meats. Use a food processor to slice the potatoes quickly.

4 new potatoes, unpeeled and sliced

Salt and freshly ground pepper to taste

3 tomatoes, peeled (page 30) and sliced

1 yellow onion, sliced and separated into rings

2 cloves garlic, minced

1 teaspoon snipped fresh thyme, or ½ teaspoon dried thyme, crumbled

1 tablespoon chopped fresh basil, or ¾ teaspoon dried basil, crumbled

2 tablespoons chopped parsley

½ cup chicken broth

1 tablespoon butter or margarine, cut up

1 cup grated Cheddar cheese

Preheat oven to 350°F. In an lightly oiled or sprayed 7½- by 11¾-inch baking dish arrange half of the potatoes. Sprinkle with salt and pepper. Add half of the tomatoes and onion rings, garlic, and herbs. Repeat layers. Pour broth evenly over vegetables. Dot with butter.

Bake, covered, 50 minutes. Sprinkle cheese over the top and bake, uncovered, until the vegetables are tender crisp and the cheese is melted, about 10 minutes longer. Serve immediately.

Greek Zucchini Pancakes

This is a perfect vegetable side dish to serve with grilled lamb chops or Grilled Butterflied Leg of Lamb (page 238).

2 large zucchini, grated
1 teaspoon salt
1 large egg
1/2 cup crumbled feta cheese
3 green onions including some tender green tops, sliced
1 clove garlic, minced
1/2 teaspoon dried oregano, crumbled
3 tablespoons flour
2 tablespoons pine nuts
Freshly ground pepper to taste
1 tablespoon vegetable oil, for frying

In a colander mix zucchini and salt, tossing lightly. Let stand about 1 hour to drain, tossing several times. Squeeze out moisture with fingers and pat dry with paper towels.

In a bowl beat egg. Add zucchini, cheese, onion, garlic, oregano, flour, pine nuts, and pepper, and mix well.

On a large plate divide zucchini mixture into fourths. Shape into patties.

In a nonstick skillet warm oil. Fry patties until golden brown, about 5 minutes on each side. Add more oil as needed. Transfer to a warmed plate and serve immediately.

Pasta

plus Grains and Legumes

Over the past decade, Americans
have doubled their consumption of
pasta. New and interesting
shapes and variations are appearing
on the market and have become the
basis of many creative light meals
and side dishes. Pasta is a
complex carbohydrate and
is often called
a high-energy food. It is
low in fat and sodium,
which appeals to the
health-conscious
dieter. Pasta is
inexpensive and quick and
easy to prepare.

Pasta Basics

Pasta comes in two forms, dried and fresh. Dried pasta can be found in packages or in bulk in many shapes and colors. It will last indefinitely stored in a cool, dry place. Fresh pasta can be found in the refrigerated section of most supermarkets or pasta shops. It is highly perishable. Refrigerated in an airtight wrap, it may be kept for up to four days or frozen for up to one month.

How much pasta to cook? The rule of thumb is that one pound of pasta serves eight for a side dish and four for a main course. You may adjust these amounts, depending on other ingredients added.

Cook pasta in a large pan, uncovered, in a generous amount of boiling water. Adding salt to the water is a personal choice. Allow four quarts of water for each pound of pasta. Add pasta to the boiling water, stirring occasionally. The pan must be large enough to permit the strands to roll around freely and cook evenly. Keep the water at a gentle rolling boil while cooking.

Do not overcook the pasta. Fresh pasta cooks in one to two minutes. Dried pasta takes longer; follow the package directions for the timing as shapes and sizes vary. To test for doneness, remove a strand and taste it. It should be firm to the bite—al dente—and a little chewy. Drain immediately; do not rinse the pasta under water unless it is to be used in a salad. At this point, the pasta can be returned to the pan and tossed with the sauce or other ingredients.

Serve pasta immediately. Pasta must be piping hot to be good. Place in a warmed serving dish or on warmed plates.

To store leftover plain pasta, mix with a little oil, cover, and refrigerate. To reheat pasta, drop into boiling water and stir gently for about one minute.

Grain Basics

While the pasta market was exploding, rice and other grains took a back seat. Now, with the introduction of some new grains and a revival of some of the old, they are becoming popular again. Grains are versatile, inexpensive, and a good source of protein and carbohydrates.

Rice is an ancient staple of many cultures and is probably the most popular of all the grains; there are some forty thousand varieties. Most rice is classified as short-grain, medium-grain, long-grain, and fragrant-grain.

Grains are available in packages or in bulk. They should be stored in the box or bag in a cool, dry place.

The different types of rice require different measurements and cooking time. Generally, rice is cooked covered with liquid until all the liquid is absorbed. One cup of raw rice makes three cups cooked and will serve four. Follow package directions for cooking rice and other grains. Some grains require washing, so read directions carefully.

Legume Basics

Legumes are dried beans, peas, lentils, soybeans, and peanuts. They are rich in protein and other nutrients and are often served as a meat substitute. They also make wonderful soups.

- Legumes are sold in packages and in bulk. Store in their packages for up to one year.

- Wash beans thoroughly and discard any withered beans or small pebbles.

- Most legumes (except lentils and split peas) require overnight soaking to rehydrate them. If you are short of time, use the "quick soak" method: Boil beans in water to cover for two minutes, cover, remove from heat, and let stand for one hour. Drain and proceed with recipe.

- Do not salt until after beans have cooked (salt toughens them).

- Dried beans triple in volume as they cook.

191

Seafood and Mushroom Pasta with Basil Pesto

A satisfying light meal and easy to prepare; seafood can vary by choice and availability. Serve with a mixed green salad and crusty, warm bread.

3 tablespoons vegetable oil
½ pound mushrooms, sliced
½ cup chopped red bell pepper
¾ pound scallops
¾ pound medium shrimp, peeled and deveined
12 ounces fresh fettuccini
¼ teaspoon salt
Freshly ground pepper to taste
Basil Pesto, homemade (recipe follows) or purchased

In a skillet over medium heat warm 2 tablespoons oil. Add mushrooms and red pepper and sauté until soft, about 5 minutes. Remove to a plate and set aside. Add remaining oil to the pan and sauté scallops for 2 minutes. Add shrimp and sauté until scallops are opaque and shrimp are pink, about 2 minutes longer.

Meanwhile, in a large pot of boiling water, cook pasta about 2 minutes. Drain and return to pan. Add mushrooms, red bell pepper, seafood, salt, pepper, and Basil Pesto to taste and toss gently. Serve immediately on warm plates.

Basil Pesto

2 cups firmly packed fresh
  basil leaves, washed
  and dried
2 parsley sprigs
2 cloves garlic, cut up
3 tablespoons pine nuts
1/4 cup freshly grated
  Parmesan cheese
1/4 teaspoon salt
Freshly ground pepper
  to taste
3 tablespoons olive oil

In a food processor or blender place all ingredients except oil. Process until minced. With motor running, slowly pour oil through the tube and blend. Scrape down sides of bowl with spatula. Transfer to a bowl, cover, and refrigerate until ready to use. Bring to room temperature before mixing with pasta.

Makes about 1/2 cup

Pasta and Thick Tomato Sauce with Basil and Pine Nuts

A meatless pasta, this is a tomato-based dish accented with basil and pine nuts.

12 ounces ziti or
   mostaccioli, cooked and
   drained
2 cups Thick Tomato
   Sauce (recipe follows)
¼ cup toasted pine nuts
   (see note)
¼ cup slivered basil leaves
Freshly grated Parmesan
   cheese, for topping

In a large warmed bowl toss pasta with Thick Tomato Sauce, pine nuts, and basil. Sprinkle with Parmesan cheese and serve immediately.

Note: To toast pine nuts, preheat oven to 350°F. Spread nuts on a baking sheet and bake until golden brown, 3 to 4 minutes. Watch carefully as they burn easily.

Thick Tomato Sauce

This is one tomato sauce guaranteed not to get watery.

1 tablespoon olive oil
½ cup chopped yellow onion
2 large cloves garlic, minced
1 can (14½ ounces) whole tomatoes with juice, cut up
½ can (3 ounces) tomato paste (see note)
2 tablespoons red wine or water
¼ teaspoon sugar
½ teaspoon salt
½ teaspoon dried oregano, crumbled
½ teaspoon dried basil, crumbled
¼ teaspoon dried marjoram, crumbled
Freshly ground pepper to taste

In a saucepan over medium heat warm oil. Sauté onion and garlic until soft, about 5 minutes. Add remaining ingredients. Simmer, uncovered, on low heat for 10 minutes.

Makes about 2 cups

Note: Leftover tomato paste may be frozen.

Pasta with Roasted Vegetables

Roasted vegetables add an intense flavor to this pasta dish. Serve with a tossed green salad for a light supper.

1 small eggplant (about 1 pound), unpeeled and cut into 1-inch pieces, about 5 cups

1 red pepper, seeded and cut into 1-inch pieces

1 large zucchini, unpeeled and sliced into 3/8-inch pieces

1/2 yellow onion, chopped

4 to 5 tablespoons olive oil

Salt and freshly ground pepper to taste

3 tomatoes, seeded and chopped

4 cloves garlic, chopped

1/3 cup chopped fresh basil, or 1 teaspoon dried basil, crumbled

1/4 cup chopped parsley

1/4 cup freshly grated Parmesan cheese, plus more for topping

8 ounces (about 2 1/2 cups) penne or mostaccioli, cooked

Preheat oven to 450°F. In a large baking dish or jelly-roll pan toss eggplant, red pepper, zucchini, and onion with 2 tablespoons oil. Season with salt and pepper. Roast in oven 10 minutes. Add tomatoes, garlic, basil, parsley, and 2 more tablespoons oil and mix with other vegetables. Roast about 12 minutes longer. Stir in 1/4 cup Parmesan cheese. Transfer vegetables and juices to a saucepan and keep warm, covered, over low heat.

Meanwhile, in a large pot of boiling water, cook pasta until al dente, 10 to 13 minutes. Drain and transfer to a large warmed bowl. Toss pasta with vegetable mixture. Add more oil if desired. Sprinkle with Parmesan cheese and serve immediately.

Vermicelli and Sausage

This main-dish pasta topped with sausage makes an attractive presentation.

4 to 6 Italian sausages (about 1¼ pounds)

¼ cup water

8 ounces dry vermicelli, cooked and drained

2 tomatoes, seeded and chopped

½ cup chopped parsley

¼ cup chopped fresh basil, or ¾ teaspoon dried basil, crumbled

½ teaspoon salt

Freshly ground pepper to taste

¼ cup freshly grated Parmesan cheese

3 to 4 tablespoons olive oil

Parsley sprigs, for garnish

In a large nonstick skillet, heat sausage in water until it boils. Reduce temperature to low, cover, and cook 5 minutes. Remove cover and cook over medium-low heat until water evaporates and sausages are browned, about 15 minutes, turning several times. Keep warm in pan.

In a large saucepan combine drained pasta with tomatoes, parsley, basil, salt, pepper, Parmesan cheese, and oil and mix well. Place over medium-low heat and warm thoroughly, about 2 minutes, tossing several times. Transfer to a large warmed platter.

Slice each sausage diagonally into 4 pieces and lay on top of pasta. Garnish with parsley and serve immediately.

Pasta with Red Bell Pepper, Mushrooms, and Zucchini

Low in calories and cholesterol, this dish can be served as a light entrée along with a green salad and garlic bread.

1 tablespoon vegetable oil

½ red bell pepper, seeded, sliced into ⅜-inch strips, and strips halved

6 green onions including some tender green tops, sliced

¼ pound mushrooms, sliced

1 zucchini, sliced lengthwise, then sliced into ⅜-inch pieces

2 cloves garlic, minced

1 can (14½ ounces) diced tomatoes in purée

Salt and freshly ground pepper to taste

4 or 5 fresh basil leaves, chopped, or ¾ teaspoon dried basil

8 ounces fresh mostaccioli, cooked and drained

1 tablespoon olive oil or butter (optional)

⅓ cup freshly grated Parmesan cheese, plus more for topping

¼ cup chopped parsley

In a large nonstick skillet, warm oil on medium heat. Add bell pepper, onions, mushrooms, zucchini, and garlic and sauté until tender crisp, 6 to 8 minutes. Add tomatoes, salt, pepper, and basil and cook until flavors are blended, stirring occasionally, about 20 minutes.

Toss with pasta, oil, cheese, and parsley and mix well. Transfer to a warm platter and serve immediately. Top with more Parmesan cheese.

Angel Hair Pasta with Gorgonzola Sauce

The melted cheeses combined with milk form a creamy sauce to toss with hot pasta. Serve with Spinach and Shrimp Salad (page 67). Gorgonzola (from Italy) is one of the three great blue cheeses, along with Roquefort (from France), and Stilton (from England), each named for its village of origin. Gorgonzola is semisoft, crumbly, yellowish white, and marbled with green mold. It is sharp in flavor and has a strong bouquet. There are good domestic blues too—Oregon Blue, Maytag Blue (from Iowa), Stella Blue (from Wisconsin), and Minnesota Blue.

4 ounces light cream cheese, cut up

4 ounces Gorgonzola cheese, crumbled

1 tablespoon freshly grated Parmesan cheese

1 clove garlic, minced

1¾ to 2 cups milk (see note)

¼ teaspoon salt

⅛ teaspoon white pepper

12 ounces angel hair pasta, cooked and drained

Parmesan cheese, for topping

In a saucepan over medium heat place cheeses, garlic, and milk. Stir until cheese is melted and sauce is smooth. Reduce heat and cook until slightly thickened, stirring occasionally, about 5 minutes longer. Season with salt and pepper.

Toss with pasta and place in a warmed bowl. Sprinkle with Parmesan cheese.

Note: For a richer sauce use half-and-half.

Chicken, Mushrooms, and Tomato Linguini

A main-dish pasta, this will serve as a light supper or lunch. Accompany it with Spinach, Pear, and Walnut Salad with Raspberry Vinaigrette (page 48) and French bread, and Lemon Drop Cookies (page 282) for dessert.

4 boned and skinned chicken breast halves
2 parsley sprigs
1/4 teaspoon salt
Water
1 tablespoon olive oil
1/2 cup chopped onion
2 cloves garlic, minced
4 to 6 mushrooms, sliced
2 tomatoes, seeded and chopped
1/4 cup chopped fresh basil leaves, or 1 teaspoon dried basil, crumbled
1/4 teaspoon salt
Freshly ground pepper to taste
12 ounces linguini, cooked
Freshly grated Parmesan cheese

In a saucepan over medium-low heat, simmer chicken with parsley sprigs in salted water to cover, until chicken turns white, about 10 minutes. Remove to a plate and set aside to cool. Discard parsley and water.

Rinse the saucepan; add oil and warm over medium heat. Add onion, garlic, and mushrooms and sauté until vegetables are soft, about 5 minutes.

Cut chicken into 1/2-inch strips and add to vegetables along with tomatoes, basil, salt, and pepper and simmer until flavors are blended, about 5 minutes longer. Toss with linguini, sprinkle with Parmesan cheese and serve immediately.

Acini di Pepe and Mushrooms

Acini di pepe is a small round pasta found in the dried pasta section of most supermarkets. It looks like couscous but has a different flavor and texture. It can be served plain or with mushrooms as in this recipe.

3 cups water
¼ teaspoon salt
1 cup acini di pepe
1 tablespoon butter or margarine
6 green onions including some tender green tops, sliced
1 clove garlic, minced
6 mushrooms, sliced
¼ cup chopped fresh basil, or ½ teaspoon dried basil, crumbled
¼ teaspoon salt
Freshly ground pepper to taste

In a large saucepan over high heat bring water and salt to a boil. Add acini, reduce heat, and cook, uncovered, until tender, 10 to 12 minutes. Drain if necessary.

Meanwhile, in a skillet melt butter over medium heat. Add onions, garlic, and mushrooms, and sauté until vegetables are soft, about 5 minutes. Add vegetables to acini di pepe and mix well. Season with basil, salt, and pepper. Serve immediately or transfer to an ovenproof dish and keep warm in a 300°F oven for up to 30 minutes.

Orzo with Parmesan Cheese

Orzo is a small, oval pasta that can be served as an alternate to a rice dish. The addition of cheese gives this dish extra flavor and creaminess.

1 tablespoon butter or margarine

6 green onions including some tender green tops, sliced

1 large clove garlic, minced

1 cup orzo

2 cups chicken broth

1/3 cup freshly grated Parmesan cheese

1/4 cup chopped fresh parsley

Salt and freshly ground pepper to taste

In a saucepan over medium heat melt butter. Add onion and garlic and sauté until vegetables are soft, about 5 minutes. Stir in orzo. Add chicken broth and bring to a boil. Reduce heat to low and cook, covered, until liquid is absorbed, 20 to 25 minutes.

Add cheese, parsley, salt, and pepper. Cook until cheese is melted, stirring once, about 5 minutes longer. Serve immediately or place in a lightly oiled or sprayed 2-quart casserole and keep warm in a warm oven up to 30 minutes.

Pasta and Grain Pilaf

The combination of grains and pasta results in an interesting taste and a chewy texture. This is a wonderful side dish with any meat or fish entrée.

1 tablespoon butter or margarine

½ cup chopped yellow onion

2 cloves garlic, minced

½ cup long-grain brown rice

½ cup pearl barley, sorted and rinsed

½ cup orzo

3 cups chicken broth

¼ cup chopped fresh basil, or ¾ teaspoon dried basil, crumbled

1 tablespoon chopped fresh thyme, or ½ teaspoon dried thyme, crumbled

¼ teaspoon salt

Freshly ground pepper to taste

¼ cup chopped parsley

In a saucepan over medium heat melt butter. Add onion and garlic and sauté until soft, about 5 minutes. Add rice, barley, and orzo and stir until grains and pasta are coated. Add chicken broth, basil, thyme, salt, and pepper.

Bring to a boil, then reduce heat and cook, covered, until liquid is absorbed, 45 to 50 minutes. Add parsley and fluff with a fork. Serve immediately.

Bulgur and Almond Pilaf

Bulgur is whole wheat that has been steamed, dried, and crushed. The toasted almonds add a chewy texture and nutty flavor to this dish, which is perfect to serve with your favorite meat, especially lamb.

¼ cup slivered almonds
1 tablespoon vegetable oil
½ cup chopped yellow
   onion
1 cup bulgur
2 cups chicken broth
Salt and freshly ground
   pepper to taste
¼ cup chopped parsley

In a small nonstick dry skillet over medium high heat stir almonds until toasted, 2 to 3 minutes, then set aside. In a saucepan over medium heat warm oil. Sauté onion until soft, about 5 minutes. Add bulgur and stir to coat. Add chicken broth and bring to a boil.

Cover, and cook over low heat until liquid is absorbed and bulgur is tender, about 20 minutes. Add salt, pepper, parsley, and nuts and mix well. Let stand, covered, 5 minutes before serving.

Couscous with Pine Nuts

Couscous is a tiny grainlike pasta made from semolina flour and is the basis of many North African dishes. It is gaining in popularity because it has no fat, no cholesterol, and takes only minutes to prepare. It has a mild, fluffy texture and is perfect to serve with stew to absorb the juices.

1 1/2 cups chicken broth or water

1 1/2 cups couscous

6 green onions including some tender green tops, sliced

1/4 cup toasted pine nuts (page 194)

1/4 cup chopped parsley

2 tablespoons chopped fresh mint leaves

1 tablespoon fresh lemon juice

2 to 3 tablespoons butter or margarine (optional)

Salt and freshly ground pepper to taste

In a small pan over high heat bring chicken broth or water to a boil. Stir in couscous and onions. Remove from heat, cover, and let stand, about 5 minutes.

Stir in pine nuts, parsley, mint, lemon juice, butter (if desired), and salt and pepper and fluff with a fork. Serve immediately or keep warm in a pan over hot water until ready to serve.

Pink Rice

This is my version of a colorful rice dish we were served in Mexico.
It makes a good accompaniment to a Mexican dinner.

1 tablespoon vegetable oil
1/2 yellow onion, chopped
1 clove garlic, chopped
3 small canned peeled
  tomatoes, drained
1 cup white long-grain
  rice
1 1/2 cups chicken broth
1/4 teaspoon ground
  cumin
1/4 teaspoon salt
Freshly ground pepper
  to taste
1/4 cup chopped cilantro
  or parsley, for topping

In a saucepan over medium heat warm oil. Add onion and garlic and sauté until tender, about 5 minutes. With a slotted spoon transfer onion and garlic to a food processor or blender, add tomatoes, and process until smooth. In the same saucepan stir rice until coated with oil.

Add broth, cumin, salt, pepper, and tomato mixture, and bring to a boil. Reduce temperature to low and cook, covered, until rice is tender, about 20 minutes. Fluff with a fork and transfer to a warm bowl. Sprinkle cilantro or parsley on top and serve immediately.

Rice and Mushroom Pilaf

A good side dish to serve with more assertive foods, this can be cooked on top of the stove or baked in the oven.

1 tablespoon butter or margarine

1 tablespoon vegetable oil

1/2 cup chopped yellow onion

1 clove garlic, minced

1/2 pound mushrooms, sliced

1 cup long-grain white rice

2 cups chicken broth or water

1/4 teaspoon dried thyme, crumbled

1/4 cup freshly grated Parmesan cheese

2 tablespoons chopped parsley

Salt and freshly ground pepper to taste

In a saucepan melt butter with oil over medium heat. Add vegetables and sauté until soft, about 5 minutes. Add rice and stir to coat. Add broth and thyme and bring to a boil, reduce heat to low, and cook, covered, until liquid is absorbed, about 20 minutes. Add Parmesan cheese, parsley, salt, and pepper. Stir until cheese melts, then serve in a warm bowl.

To bake, preheat oven to 350°F. Place in a lightly oiled or sprayed 2-quart baking dish. Cover and bake until liquid is absorbed, about 50 minutes. Add Parmesan cheese, parsley, salt, and pepper and stir until cheese melts.

Orange, Rice, and Barley Pilaf

This orange-flavored rice and barley side dish is a great way to add grains to your diet. It is a good complementary dish to serve with Orange-Thyme Lamb Chops (page 236).

1 cup fresh orange juice

1 cup chicken broth

1 cup long-grain brown rice

¼ cup barley, sorted and rinsed

¼ cup dry white wine

¼ teaspoon dried thyme, crumbled

¼ teaspoon salt

Freshly ground pepper to taste

¼ cup chopped parsley

¼ cup chopped walnuts (optional)

In a saucepan over medium-high heat, bring orange juice and broth to a boil. Stir in rice and barley. Add wine and seasonings, except parsley. Reduce heat to low and simmer, covered, until liquid is absorbed and rice and barley are tender, about 50 minutes. Add parsley and nuts and fluff with a fork. Serve immediately.

Basmati Rice with Nuts and Spices

SERVES 4 AS A SIDE DISH

Basmati rice is grown in the foothills of the Himalayan Mountains and is known for its fragrant aroma, nutlike flavor, and firm consistency. You can serve it plain or with exotic spices and nuts as called for in this recipe. Grown in America, it is called Texmati, and comes in both white and brown varieties.

2 tablespoons butter or margarine

1/2 cup chopped yellow onion

2 cloves garlic, minced

1/4 cup slivered almonds

1/4 cup coarsely chopped cashews

1 cup basmati rice, rinsed

2 cups chicken broth or water

1/2 teaspoon curry powder

1/4 teaspoon ground cardamom

1/4 teaspoon ground coriander

1/2 cup chopped parsley

1 tablespoon lemon juice

1/4 cup golden raisins (optional)

Salt and freshly ground pepper to taste

In a saucepan over medium heat melt butter. Add onion and garlic and sauté until soft, about 5 minutes. Add nuts and rice and stir to coat. Add broth and spices and bring to a boil.

Reduce heat, cover, and simmer until all liquid is absorbed, about 20 minutes. Add parsley, lemon juice, raisins, salt, and pepper, and fluff with a fork.

Wild Rice Plus

The earthy, intense flavor of wild rice is balanced with the bland flavor of white rice for an interesting combination.

1 to 2 tablespoons butter or margarine

1 cup chopped yellow onion

1/2 cup wild rice, rinsed thoroughly

1 cup water

1 cup chicken broth

1/4 teaspoon salt

1/2 cup long-grain white rice

Freshly ground pepper to taste

1/4 cup chopped parsley

In a large saucepan over medium heat melt 1 tablespoon butter. Sauté onion until soft, about 5 minutes. Add wild rice and stir to coat. Add water, chicken broth, and salt. Bring to a boil; reduce heat and simmer, covered, 25 minutes. Stir in white rice and simmer, covered, until rice is soft and liquid is absorbed, about 20 minutes longer. Add pepper and parsley and fluff with a fork. Serve immediately.

Oriental Rice

A complementary side dish to serve with Asian-style entrées.

1 tablespoon butter or
 margarine
1 cup sliced celery
1/2 cup chopped yellow
 onion
3/4 cup long-grain white
 rice
1 can (6 ounces) water
 chestnuts, drained and
 sliced (optional)
2 cups chicken broth
1 to 2 tablespoons soy
 sauce to taste
Salt and freshly ground
 pepper to taste
2 or 3 green onions
 including some tender
 green tops, sliced, for
 garnish

In a saucepan over medium heat melt butter. Add celery and onion and sauté until vegetables are soft, about 6 minutes. Stir in rice and chestnuts, if using. Add broth and bring to a boil, reduce heat to low, cover, and cook until rice is tender and liquid is absorbed, about 20 minutes. Add soy, salt, and pepper and mix well. Place in a warmed bowl and top with green onions. Serve immediately.

Variation: Sauté 1 cup snap peas with celery and onions.

Savory Brown Rice

Brown rice is unpolished with only the outer hull removed, resulting in a darker color, a chewy texture, and more fiber. (White rice is milled to remove hull, germ, and most of the bran.) Brown rice takes longer to cook than white rice. This makes a nice side dish to serve with meats or seafood.

2 tablespoons butter or margarine

1/2 onion, chopped

1/2 green or red bell pepper, chopped

1 celery stalk, sliced

1 cup long-grain brown rice

2 cups chicken or vegetable broth or water

1/4 teaspoon dried thyme, crumbled

1/4 teaspoon dried marjoram, crumbled

1/4 teaspoon dry mustard

1/4 teaspoon salt

Freshly ground pepper to taste

1/4 cup minced parsley

In a saucepan over medium heat melt butter. Add vegetables and sauté until slightly soft, about 6 minutes. Stir in rice. Add broth and seasonings, except parsley, and bring to a boil. Reduce heat to low and cook, covered, until liquid is absorbed, 45 to 50 minutes. Stir in parsley and serve immediately.

Corn–Chile–Rice Casserole

*Corn is a staple in Mexico and appears in many Mexican dishes.
The peppers add flavor and color to the rice. This recipe serves a
large group and can be made ahead and baked later.*

1 tablespoon vegetable oil

1 cup chopped
 red bell pepper

1 cup chopped
 yellow onion

2 cups long-grain rice

2 cups water

1 can (14½ ounces)
 chicken broth

1 teaspoon ground cumin

½ teaspoon salt

Freshly ground pepper
 to taste

1 cup fresh corn, or frozen
 corn, thawed

2 or 3 jalapeño peppers,
 chopped, or 1 can
 (4 ounces) diced chiles,
 drained

½ cup light sour cream

1½ cups grated Monterey
 Jack cheese

In a large saucepan warm oil over
medium heat. Sauté bell pepper and
onion until soft, about 5 minutes.
Add rice and stir to coat. Stir in water,
broth, cumin, salt, and pepper. Bring
to a boil, then reduce heat and cook,
covered, until liquid is absorbed,
about 25 minutes. Remove lid and cool
slightly. Gently stir in corn, chiles, and
sour cream.

Preheat oven to 350°F. Transfer to a
lightly oiled or sprayed 4-quart casserole
and top with cheese. Bake, uncovered,
until heated through and cheese is
melted, about 20 minutes. (If made
ahead, bring to room temperature
before baking.)

Basic Polenta

Polenta is a cornmeal specialty of Italy. It can be served as a hearty breakfast mush or, combined with other ingredients, served as a main course or side dish. Directions follow for boiled (soft or basic), baked, fried, and grilled polenta.

1 cup yellow cornmeal
3½ cups cold water
¼ teaspoon salt
¼ cup freshly grated
  Parmesan cheese
1 tablespoon butter or
  margarine

In a bowl mix cornmeal with 1 cup water. In a saucepan over high heat combine remaining 2½ cups water and salt and bring to a boil. Slowly pour cornmeal mixture into boiling water, stirring constantly. Reduce heat to low and simmer, uncovered, stirring constantly until thick and smooth, about 3 minutes. Remove from heat. Stir in Parmesan cheese and butter. Immediately spoon onto plates or bowls and serve.

Polenta Variations

For additional flavor, chicken broth may be substituted for water.

To fry or grill, turn Basic Polenta into a 7½- by 11¾-inch lightly oiled or sprayed baking dish. Cover and chill until firm, several hours. To fry, cut chilled polenta into 2- by 3-inch pieces. In a large, nonstick skillet over medium heat cook polenta in 2 to 3 tablespoons butter until golden and crisp, 5 to 6 minutes on each side. To grill, cut chilled polenta into 2- by 3-inch pieces. Brush grill well with vegetable oil and grill until warm and grill marks are visible, 6 to 8 minutes on each side.

To bake plain, preheat oven to 350°F. Turn Basic Polenta (unchilled) into a lightly oiled or sprayed /½- by 11¾-inch baking dish. Sprinkle with cheese, if desired. Bake, uncovered, until firm, about 20 minutes. Let stand 5 minutes, then cut into squares and serve immediately.

To bake with sauce, cover Basic Polenta with 1 cup Thick Tomato Sauce (page 195) or 1 can (8 ounces) tomato sauce. Sprinkle with Parmesan cheese, if desired. Bake until firm and bubbly, 30 to 35 minutes. Let stand 5 to 10 minutes, then cut into squares and serve immediately.

Corn and Black Bean Polenta

Two popular foods team together in a tasty casserole for a side dish or main course.

Basic Polenta (page 214)

1 cup cooked corn, cut from 2 ears, or 1 cup frozen corn, thawed

1 can (15 ounces) black beans, rinsed, drained, and patted dry with a paper towel

1 cup chopped red bell pepper

1 can (8 ounces) tomato sauce

2 cups firmly packed, grated Monterey Jack cheese

Light sour cream, for topping

Preheat oven to 350°F. Make polenta and turn it into a lightly oiled or sprayed 7½- by 11¾-inch glass baking dish. Add a layer of corn on top of the polenta, then a layer of beans, and a layer of peppers. Pour tomato sauce over and sprinkle with cheese. Bake, uncovered, until polenta is firm and bubbly, about 30 minutes.

Let stand 5 to 10 minutes. Cut into squares and serve immediately. Pass sour cream in a bowl.

Great on the Grill

Roll out the barbecue and stay cool, eat light, and take it easy. That first grilled hamburger or steak in the spring is always a welcome change, but grilling can be done year round with the proper equipment.

Barbecues are a casual and informal way to entertain and are often spur-of-the-moment events. They encourage a relaxed mood as guests serve themselves and often help with the barbecuing. Almost an entire meal can be grilled at the same time, thus saving time, energy, and clean up.

There are several kinds and styles of grills on the market—charcoal, gas, and electric. It is important to read the manufacturers' directions carefully to understand the technique and safety precautions. Once the technique is learned, and with practice, grilling can be done with ease.

Grilling Basics

Equipment

Charcoal briquets, if using, should be of the best quality.

Gas for the gas grill; if possible, keep an extra tank on hand for emergencies.

Barbecue tools: Longhandled tongs and spatula for turning food, brush or spoon for applying marinade, wire cleaning brush, insulated mitt, meat and oven thermometers, skewers, a hinged wire rack, and grilling grid. (A grilling grid is a grid with holes designed to be placed directly on the grill. It works well for kabobs and fish and can be purchased at most cook stores and barbecue departments.)

A small table nearby to hold tools, marinades, serving dishes, salt and pepper, and water to extinguish any flames caused by fat drippings makes grilling more convenient.

Preparing the Grill

Follow manufacturer's recommendations for using briquets. An electric coil starter or metal chimney is recommended for lighting briquets. If using charcoal lighter fluid, allow time for it to be totally consumed. (Do not use other substances not intended for barbecuing, as they may leave an aftertaste and can also be dangerous.) Preheat a charcoal grill for 20 to 30 minutes until coals are hot and gray.

Preheat a gas grill for 10 minutes; electric grills for 3 to 4 minutes.

Clean grill rack thoroughly with a wire brush.

Brush grill rack with vegetable oil when cooking directly on grill.

For an extra-smoky flavor, soak a few wood chips in water for about an hour, drain, and add to coals the last 15 minutes of cooking. Fresh herbs or citrus peel can also be added to the coals for flavor and fragrance.

Do not grill indoors unless you are using equipment designed specifically for this purpose.

Marinades and Bastes

Marinades enhance the flavor of grilled food, seal in the juices so food won't dry out and, in some cases, tenderize meats. Marinate food in a glass, stainless-steel, or non-reactive container. Cover and marinate meats in the refrigerator following recipe directions. Remove from refrigerator 30 minutes before grilling. Use leftover marinade to baste food while grilling.

Never serve leftover marinade that has come in contact with raw meat unless it has been boiled to destroy bacteria.

Do not marinate seafood for long periods of time in a citrus marinade because it will begin to "cook."

Bastes are brushed on food while it is being grilled for added flavor and to keep food from drying out.

Grilling

Place steaks, chops, and hamburgers directly on an oiled grill rack over hot coals 4 to 6 inches from heat. Turn meat several times until done to your taste. Salt and pepper after cooking.

Place chicken directly on prepared grill rack or in an oiled foil pan or glass baking dish. The pan method keeps the chicken from burning and charring, especially when a sweet barbecue sauce is added. For a crisp result, remove chicken from pan and place on grill the last 10 minutes of cooking, turning several times. Chicken pieces usually take 1 hour to cook, breasts about 30 minutes, and whole chickens 1¼ to 1½ hours, depending on size.

Grill fish steaks and fillets in an oiled or sprayed hinged wire rack, turning several times. The rack keeps the fish in one piece and makes it easier to turn. Cook 8 to 10 minutes to the inch measured at the thickest part. Fish is done when flesh is opaque and flakes easily when tested with a fork. Do not overcook; the fish will be dry and tasteless. Fish continues to cook after it has been removed from the heat.

Grill vegetables and fruit on a prepared grill rack or in a sprayed, hinged wire rack.

New York Steaks with Sautéed Mushrooms

SERVES 4

Grilling is an ideal way to cook these full-flavored steaks. Top with Sautéed Mushrooms and serve with Angel Hair Pasta and Gorgonzola Sauce (page 199), Garden Salad with Sevé French Dressing (page 52), and Strawberry Shortcake (page 274). For a special occasion, serve Roasted Red Bell Pepper Crostini with Feta Cheese (page 8) as an hors d'oeuvre.

4 New York steaks
(8 ounces each, 1-inch thick)
Salt and freshly ground pepper to taste
Sautéed Mushrooms (recipe follows)

Prepare grill and oil with vegetable oil. Place steaks on grill over medium heat. Grill 5 to 6 minutes on each side for medium rare. Season with salt and pepper. Serve with Sautéed Mushrooms over the top or on the side.

Sautéed Mushrooms

3 tablespoons butter or margarine
1 pound mushrooms (about 20), sliced
2 cloves garlic, minced
4 green onions including some tender green tops, sliced
¼ cup dry white wine
2 teaspoons Dijon mustard
Salt and freshly ground pepper to taste

In a skillet melt butter over medium heat. Add mushrooms, garlic, and onions and sauté until tender, about 5 minutes. Add wine, mustard, salt, and pepper. Reduce heat and simmer until flavors are blended, about 5 minutes.

Serves 4

Marinated Flank Steak

If you have a craving for beef, flank steak is a great choice because it is relatively low in fat but is full of flavor. Serve with Spinach Salad with Mushrooms, Blue Cheese, and Bacon (page 57), Plank Potatoes (page 173), Grilled Corn on the Cob (page 254), baguette slices, and ice cream with Blueberry Sauce (page 288).

1 flank steak (1½ to 2
    pounds)
Flank Steak Marinade
    (recipe follows)

Place steak in a large baking dish. Pour marinade over, cover, and refrigerate for several hours, turning several times. Bring to room temperature before grilling.

Prepare grill and oil with vegetable oil. Remove steak from marinade. Place steak on grill and grill until steak is medium rare, about 7 minutes on each side (depending on thickness.) Transfer steak to a cutting board and let stand 5 minutes to absorb juices. Slice meat diagonally and transfer to a platter.

Flank Steak Marinade

2 tablespoons red wine
    vinegar
2 tablespoons soy sauce
1 tablespoon vegetable oil
1 teaspoon Worcestershire
    sauce
2 cloves garlic, minced
Dash Tabasco sauce
1/4 teaspoon dried basil,
    crumbled
1/4 teaspoon dried
    rosemary, crumbled
Freshly ground pepper
    to taste

In a large baking dish stir all
ingredients together.

Makes about 1/3 cup

Bourbon Beef Tenderloin with Grilled Tomato Halves

SERVES 8

It is necessary to have a covered barbecue for this recipe, which is the centerpiece of this company dinner. Serve with Beer Cheese Spread (page 11) and crackers, Wild Rice Plus (page 210), garlic bread, and Deep-dish Berry Pie (page 262).

1 whole beef tenderloin (about 4 pounds)

Bourbon Baste (recipe follows)

Grilled Tomato Halves (recipe follows)

Parsley sprigs, for garnish

Horseradish Sauce (page 135)

Prepare grill. Place meat in a foil pan and spread with baste. Place on the grill and cook with lid closed until meat thermometer registers 150°F for medium rare, about 1 hour and 15 minutes. (If necessary add ¼ cup water to pan to keep meat moist.)

Remove from grill and let stand 10 minutes before slicing. Grill tomato halves. Transfer meat to a platter and arrange tomato halves around meat. Garnish with parsley sprigs and serve immediately with Horseradish Sauce.

Bourbon Baste

2 tablespoons bourbon
3 tablespoons soy sauce
1 tablespoon Dijon
   mustard
1 tablespoon vegetable oil
1 tablespoon honey
1 teaspoon prepared
   horseradish
2 cloves garlic, minced
Freshly ground pepper
   to taste

In a small bowl stir together baste ingredients.

Makes about ½ cup

Grilled Tomato Halves

4 large firm tomatoes,
   unpeeled and halved
Vegetable oil, for
   brushing tomatoes
Salt and freshly ground
   pepper to taste
Freshly grated Parmesan
   cheese
2 teaspoons dried basil,
   crumbled
3 tablespoons chopped
   parsley

Brush tomato halves with oil, top and bottom. While the meat is resting, place tomatoes, cut-side down, on grill. Cook until tomatoes are warm but still firm, about 5 minutes. Turn tomatoes with a spatula. Sprinkle with salt, pepper, Parmesan cheese, basil, and parsley. Continue cooking until cheese is melted, 1 to 2 minutes longer. Serve immediately.

Serves 8

Beef and Vegetable Kabobs

Here the complete entrée is cooked on skewers and then arranged on a platter for an appealing and impressive presentation. Serve with a salad of mixed greens with Italian Dressing (page 56), Pasta and Thick Tomato Sauce with Basil and Pine Nuts (page 194), and warm sourdough bread.

1½ pounds top sirloin, cut into 1½-inch cubes

Red Wine Marinade (recipe follows)

1 large head garlic, separated and peeled

1 red or green bell pepper, cut into 1-inch pieces

12 mushrooms, stemmed

1 large zucchini, cut into 1-inch slices

12 cherry tomatoes

Place meat in a large bowl and mix with marinade. Cover and marinate several hours in the refrigerator, stirring several times. Bring to room temperature.

Prepare grill. Remove meat from marinade, reserving marinade. Thread meat and vegetables onto skewers, placing garlic cloves next to meat.

Grill on oiled grill turning skewers several times and basting meat and vegetables with remaining marinade, 8 to 10 minutes for medium rare.

Red Wine Marinade

½ cup dry red wine

2 tablespoons vegetable oil

2 tablespoons soy sauce

1 teaspoon Worcestershire sauce

2 cloves garlic, minced

¼ teaspoon dry mustard

½ teaspoon salt

Freshly ground pepper to taste

In a bowl stir marinade ingredients together.

Makes about ¾ cup

Beef Roast on the Grill

*For a patio supper, marinate the meat for six hours or overnight
and then grill it along with Grilled Corn on the Cob (page 254). Serve
with sliced garden tomatoes, Roasted New Potatoes (page 174),
and frozen yogurt with Strawberry Sauce (page 288). Leftovers make
wonderful sandwiches.*

4 to 5 pounds London
   Broil beef rump roast
Soy-Wine Marinade
   (recipe follows)

Place roast in a glass baking dish. Pour
marinade over meat, cover, and refrigerate
6 hours, turning several times. Bring
to room temperature before grilling.

Prepare grill and oil with vegetable oil.
Remove meat from marinade, reserving
marinade. Place meat on grill. Grill
until medium rare, about 45 minutes,
turning several times and basting with
reserved marinade. Let stand 10 minutes
before carving.

Soy-Wine Marinade

¼ cup soy sauce
¼ cup dry red wine
1 tablespoon red wine
   vinegar
1 teaspoon Worcestershire
   sauce
2 cloves garlic, minced

In a bowl stir marinade ingredients
together.

Makes about ½ cup

Mexican-Style Pork Tenderloin

Marinate tenderloin in this zesty marinade for several hours. For a Mexican theme dinner, serve Quesadillas (page 12), Corn and Black Bean Polenta (page 216), Thick Tomato Slices with Avocado Dressing (page 58), and Frosted Chocolate Cookies (page 283).

1 pork tenderloin
(1 to 1½ pounds)
Lime-Beer Marinade
(recipe follows)
Lime wedges, for garnish

Place tenderloin in a glass baking dish. Pour marinade over and marinate, covered, in the refrigerator 4 to 6 hours, turning several times. Bring to room temperature before grilling.

Prepare grill. Remove pork from marinade, reserving marinade. Place pork in a foil pan on grill. Baste with marinade and cook with barbecue lid closed, turning several times, and basting with reserved marinade, until tender or a meat thermometer registers 150° to 160°F, about 30 minutes.

Slice and arrange on a warmed platter. Garnish with lime wedges and serve immediately.

Lime-Beer Marinade

Juice of 1 lime
1/2 cup beer, allowed to
    go flat
2 cloves garlic, minced
1/4 teaspoon dried
    oregano, crumbled
1 teaspoon chili powder
1/2 teaspoon ground cumin
1/4 teaspoon ground
    coriander
1/4 teaspoon salt
1/4 teaspoon freshly
    ground pepper
1 teaspoon Worcestershire
    sauce
2 tablespoons chopped
    cilantro or parsley

In a small bowl stir marinade
ingredients together.

Makes about ¾ cup

Dijon Pork Chops

Tender, juicy, thick pork chops straight from the grill make a wonderful warm weather entrée. Serve with Summertime Casserole (page 185), cantaloupe and watermelon slices, and Toffee Nut Bars (page 284).

4 boneless pork chops
(1-inch thick)
Dijon Baste (recipe
follows)
Salt and pepper to taste

Prepare grill. Place chops on vegetable-oiled grill. Brush with baste. Grill 8 to 10 minutes, turn and baste on other side, and grill 8 to 10 minutes longer. Season with salt and pepper and serve immediately.

Dijon Baste

2 cloves garlic, minced
2 tablespoons Dijon
mustard
3 tablespoons red wine
vinegar
1 teaspoon dried
marjoram, crumbled
1½ tablespoons
vegetable oil

In a small bowl mix garlic, mustard, vinegar, and marjoram together. Whisk in olive oil.

Makes about ¼ cup

Grilled Pork Chops with Honey Glaze

Just a brush of the glaze while they are being grilled seasons these thick chops to perfection. Start the meal with Chilled Avocado Soup (page 43), follow with Pasta with Red Bell Peppers, Mushrooms, and Zucchini (page 198), and finish with Fresh Peach Crisp (page 257) for dessert.

4 boneless pork chops
(1 to 1¼ inches thick)
Honey Glaze (recipe
follows)

Prepare grill. Place chops on a lightly oiled grill and spread half the glaze over the chops. Grill until browned, about 6 to 8 minutes. Turn chops over and spread with remaining glaze. Grill until browned and cooked through, about 6 to 8 minutes longer. Serve immediately.

Honey Glaze

1 tablespoon honey
1 tablespoon soy sauce
1 tablespoon Dijon
mustard
1 clove garlic, minced
¼ teaspoon ground
ginger
Salt and freshly ground
pepper to taste

In a cup or small bowl stir together glaze ingredients

Makes about ¼ cup

Hawaiian Pork Loin Roast

A pork loin is easy to cook and requires no carving skills. This makes an impressive company dinner when served with Spinach and Shrimp Salad (page 67) and Pasta and Grain Pilaf (page 203). End the meal with the impressive Kahlúa Chocolate Ice Cream Torte (page 270).

1 pork loin, about 4 pounds
Hawaiian Marinade (recipe follows)
Fresh pineapple, papaya, and mango slices

Place roast in a glass baking dish. Pour marinade over and marinate, covered, in the refrigerator at least 6 to 8 hours, turning once or twice. Bring to room temperature before grilling.

Prepare grill. Remove pork from marinade, reserving marinade. Place pork in a foil pan on grill. Baste with marinade and cook with barbecue lid closed, turning several times, and basting with reserved marinade, until tender or a meat thermometer registers 150° to 160°F, 1 to 1½ hours.

Let stand 10 minutes before carving, then slice and arrange on a warmed platter. Serve immediately with pineapple, papaya, and mango slices.

Hawaiian Marinade

1/2 cup soy sauce

1/4 cup sherry or dry
white wine

1/2 cup pineapple-orange
juice or orange juice

1 tablespoon red wine
vinegar

2 tablespoons honey

2 cloves, minced

1/4 teaspoon ground
ginger

1 tablespoon vegetable oil

In a bowl or cup mix all ingredients
together.

Makes about 1½ cups

Barbecued Ribs with Dry Rub and Beer Sauce

The ribs are rubbed with a dry mix for extra flavor, baked in the oven to remove most of the fat, and then finished on the grill with a Beer Sauce. For a traditional ribs dinner include baked beans and coleslaw.

6 pounds pork spareribs, cut into serving pieces
Dry Rub Mix (recipe follows)
Beer Sauce (recipe follows)

Preheat oven to 350°F. Rub ribs on all sides with Dry Rub Mix. Place ribs in a large foil roasting pan. Bake, uncovered, 1 hour. Remove from oven and pour off grease, leaving the ribs in the pan.

Prepare grill. Pour half of Beer Sauce over ribs. Place the pan on the grill and cook with lid closed, turning occasionally and brushing with remaining sauce, until ribs are tender and browned and all the sauce is used, about 45 minutes. If desired, remove ribs from pan and place directly on grill for 4 to 5 minutes for a crisper finish.

Dry Rub Mix

2 tablespoons light brown
    sugar
1 tablespoon chili powder
1 teaspoon paprika
1 teaspoon garlic powder
1 teaspoon salt
Freshly ground pepper
    to taste

In a small bowl stir together all
ingredients.

Makes ¼ cup

Beer Sauce

This is also good on chicken.

1 cup beer, allowed to
    go flat
½ can (3 ounces) tomato
    paste
½ cup soy sauce
1 teaspoon Worcestershire
    sauce
2 tablespoons Dijon
    mustard
2 cloves garlic, minced

In a small bowl whisk all ingredients
together.

Makes about 1 cup

Orange–Thyme Lamb Chops

Lamb chops are known for their tender, juicy qualities, but they are small, so allow two chops per person. They go well with Orange, Rice, and Barley Pilaf (page 208), Sauté of Summer Peas and Mushrooms (page 171), and Blueberry Pie (page 260).

8 thick lamb chops, excess
    fat trimmed
Orange-Thyme Marinade
    (recipe follows)
Salt and freshly ground
    pepper to taste
Thyme sprigs, for garnish
Orange slices, for garnish

Place chops in a glass baking dish and pour marinade over, cover, and marinate several hours in refrigerator, turning several times. Bring to room temperature before grilling.

Prepare grill. Remove chops from marinade, reserving marinade. Stand chops upright on bone end on a lightly oiled grill and grill 4 minutes. Then lay chops down on one side, brush with marinade, and grill 5 minutes; turn chops over, brush with marinade, and grill 4 minutes longer for medium. Watch carefully for flare-ups.

Season with salt and pepper and transfer to a warmed platter. Garnish with thyme sprigs and orange slices. Serve immediately.

Orange-Thyme Marinade

¼ cup orange juice
½ teaspoon orange zest
1 tablespoon olive oil
1 tablespoon fresh chopped thyme, or 1 teaspoon dried thyme, crumbled

In a cup or small bowl stir together all ingredients.

Makes about ¼ cup

Grilled Butterflied Leg of Lamb with Mint Pesto

Lamb is succulent and mild yet flavorful. Have the butcher bone and butterfly the lamb for easy grilling. To enhance the flavor, marinate overnight and scatter fresh rosemary sprigs over the coals during the last fifteen minutes of cooking time. Serve with Tzatziki (page 153), Mesclun Salad with Feta Cheese and Walnuts with Balsamic Vinaigrette Dressing (page 55), Bulgur and Almond Pilaf (page 204), and Deep-dish Berry Pie (page 262) for dessert.

1 leg of lamb (6 to 7 pounds), trimmed of excess fat, boned, and butterflied

Marinade for Lamb (recipe follows)

Mint Pesto (recipe follows)

Mint leaves, for garnish

Place lamb in a large glass baking dish and pour marinade over. Cover and refrigerate 6 to 8 hours, turning several times. Bring to room temperature before cooking.

Prepare grill. Remove meat from marinade, reserving marinade. Place on a lightly oiled grill, cut-side down, over medium coals. Grill until meat thermometer registers 145° to 150°F for medium rare, 25 to 30 minutes on each side, turning several times and basting with reserved marinade.

Let stand 10 minutes before carving. Slice across the grain in thin slices and arrange on a warmed platter. Garnish with mint leaves and serve immediately with Mint Pesto.

Marinade for Lamb

1/4 cup olive oil
Juice of 1 lemon
1/3 cup dry red wine
1 tablespoon fresh
   chopped rosemary, or
   1 teaspoon dried
   rosemary, crumbled
1 tablespoon fresh
   chopped parsley
3 tablespoons fresh
   chopped mint
3 large cloves garlic,
   chopped
1/2 teaspoon salt
Freshly ground pepper
   to taste

In a small bowl stir marinade
ingredients together.

Makes about 1/2 cup

Mint Pesto

1 cup firmly packed fresh
   mint leaves
1 cup firmly packed fresh
   parsley
2 cloves garlic, cut up
1/4 cup walnuts
1/4 cup olive oil
2 teaspoons fresh lemon
   juice
1 teaspoon sugar
1/2 teaspoon salt

In food processor or blender combine
mint, parsley, garlic, and walnuts.
Process to form a paste, scraping down
sides of the bowl, if necessary. With
motor running, gradually add oil and
blend until smooth. Add lemon juice,
sugar, and salt and process briefly to
combine. Transfer to a bowl and serve
immediately, or cover and refrigerate.
Bring to room temperature before
serving.

Makes about 1 cup

Lamb and Vegetable Kabobs

SERVES 6

Serve these Greek-inspired kabobs with Basmati Rice with Nuts and Spices (page 209), Cucumber and Red Onion Salad with Dill Dressing (page 64), and frozen fruit yogurt. Allow several hours for the lamb to marinate.

Marinade for Lamb
  (page 239)
2 1/2 pounds boneless
  lamb, cut into
  1 1/2-inch pieces
1/2 eggplant, cut into
  1-inch squares
1 red bell pepper, seeded
  and cut into 1-inch
  pieces
1 zucchini, cut into 1-inch
  slices
1/2 red onion, sliced and
  cut into 1-inch pieces
12 mushrooms
Mint leaves, for garnish

In a large bowl make marinade. Add lamb to bowl and stir to coat. Cover and refrigerate 4 to 6 hours, stirring once. Bring to room temperature before grilling. Remove meat from marinade and place on a plate. Add vegetables to marinade and stir to coat. Marinate 5 minutes.

Prepare grill. Remove vegetables from marinade, reserving marinade. Thread lamb alternately with vegetables on skewers. Place skewers on a grilling grid (see page 218) or directly on a lightly oiled grill. Grill about 12 minutes, turning several times and basting with reserved marinade. Garnish with mint leaves and serve immediately.

Grilled Drumsticks with Zesty Sauce

For an easy summer picnic serve these drumsticks with New Potato and Green Bean Salad (page 62), Grilled Corn on the Cob (page 254), garlic bread, and Cashew Brownies (page 280).

10 to 12 drumsticks, or thighs or wings
Zesty Sauce (recipe follows)

Prepare grill. Place chicken in a foil pan and spread sauce over. Place pan on grill, cover grill with lid, and cook, turning several times, until chicken juices run clear when cut with a sharp knife at the thickest part, about 45 minutes. Remove chicken from pan and place directly on the grill, again turning several times, until crisp, 4 to 5 minutes. Serve immediately.

Zesty Sauce

This bold sauce can be used on all poultry for any occasion.

1/2 cup chili sauce
Juice of 1 lemon
2 tablespoons white wine vinegar
2 tablespoons soy sauce
2 teaspoons mustard
1 tablespoon prepared horseradish sauce
1/2 teaspoon salt
Freshly ground pepper to taste

In a small bowl stir together all ingredients.

Makes about 1/2 cup

Soy–Sesame Chicken Breasts

SERVES 4

*To keep the chicken breasts moist while grilling, add a flavorful
marinade. These breasts are cooked in the marinade, then rolled in
sesame seeds and finished on the grill for a crunchy coating. Serve
with Oriental Rice (page 211) and Steamed Carrots and Zucchini
Strips (page 170).*

6 to 8 boned and skinned
   chicken breast halves
Soy Marinade (recipe
   follows)
½ cup sesame seeds

Place chicken in a foil pan and pour
marinade over chicken. Cover and
refrigerate several hours, turning occasionally. Bring to room temperature
before grilling.

Prepare grill. Place pan holding chicken
and marinade on the grill over medium
heat. Cover grill with lid and cook until
juices run clear and chicken is white
in the center, about 20 to 25 minutes.

Place seeds on a plate. Remove chicken
from pan with tongs and roll in seeds.
Oil grill with vegetable oil and place
chicken directly on grill, turning several
times, until seeds are browned and
toasted, about 2 minutes. Transfer to a
plate and serve immediately.

Soy Marinade

1/4 cup soy sauce

2 tablespoons dry white wine

1 clove garlic, minced

1 tablespoon lemon juice

1 tablespoon vegetable oil

1 tablespoon honey

1 teaspoon dry mustard

1/2 teaspoon ground ginger

1 tablespoon Worcestershire sauce

4 green onions including some tender green tops, sliced

In a bowl stir together all ingredients.

Makes about 1/2 cup

Chicken with Tangy Yogurt Sauce

SERVES 4

No wonder chicken is so popular in the summertime when it can be grilled outdoors in so many ways. This sauce with yogurt imparts a different flavor from that of the usual barbecue sauce. Serve with Vegetables Marinated with Fresh Herbs (page 66) and Blueberry-Cranberry Crisp (page 259).

1 chicken (about 3½ pounds), cut into serving pieces

Vegetable oil, for brushing on chicken

Tangy Yogurt Sauce (recipe follows)

Prepare barbecue for grilling. Place chicken in a foil pan and brush all sides with oil. Cook in foil pan on grill for 20 minutes. Pour half the sauce over the chicken and cook, turning several times and brushing with remaining sauce, until chicken is done, about 35 minutes longer. Remove chicken from pan and place directly on the grill, turning several times until crisp, 4 to 5 minutes longer.

Tangy Yogurt Sauce

½ cup catsup
¼ cup chili sauce
1 tablespoon red wine
    vinegar
2 cloves garlic, minced
1 teaspoon prepared
    mustard
¼ teaspoon salt
Freshly ground pepper
    to taste
1 tablespoon Worcester-
    shire sauce
½ cup plain nonfat yogurt

In a small bowl whisk all ingredients together until smooth.

Makes about 1¼ cups

Hot or Cold Chicken Thighs

To take to a picnic or family reunion make Greek Pasta Salad (page 70) and Buttermilk Chocolate Cake (page 278) in the morning to serve with these delicious thighs. They are equally good served hot or cold.

8 to 10 chicken thighs, skinned if desired
All-Purpose Barbecue Sauce (recipe follows)

Prepare grill. Place thighs in a foil baking pan and pour sauce over. Marinate 30 minutes at room temperature. Place pan on grill and grill until juices run clear when tested with a knife, turning once, about 45 minutes. Remove chicken from pan and place directly on grill, turning several times, until crisp, 4 to 5 minutes. Serve immediately.

All-Purpose Barbecue Sauce

This sauce is good on all poultry and on pork ribs.

1 tablespoon butter or margarine
1/2 cup dry white wine
1/2 cup catsup
1/4 teaspoon dry mustard
1 teaspoon Worcestershire sauce
1/4 cup chopped yellow onion
1 clove garlic, minced
1/2 tablespoon salt
Freshly ground pepper to taste

In a small saucepan over medium heat stir together all ingredients. Bring to a boil, reduce heat, and cook until flavors are blended, about 5 minutes. Cool slightly in pan.

Makes about 3/4 cup

Grilled Turkey Breast with Herb Baste

Turkey breast is very lean and needs a baste when grilled to keep it from drying out. Serve with Vegetable and Fresh Herb Casserole (page 186) and Strawberry Shortcake (page 274).

Turkey breast with bone in (about 4 pounds)

Herb Baste (recipe follows)

Prepare grill. Place turkey breast in a foil pan and spread on baste. Place pan holding turkey breast on grill. Grill with lid down until juices run clear and meat thermometer registers 175°F, about 1½ hours. Transfer to platter and let stand 10 minutes before carving.

Herb Baste

3 tablespoons olive oil

½ teaspoon dried thyme, crumbled

1 teaspoon dried sage, crumbled

¼ teaspoon dried basil, crumbled

¼ teaspoon salt

Dash of Tabasco sauce

2 cloves garlic, minced

In a small bowl whisk all ingredients together.

Makes about ¼ cup

Mixed Grill

This combination of meat, poultry, and vegetables is for the hearty eater. It takes a lot of watching and turning so stand by and be ready to extinguish the flames with water. Accompany this meal with Cheese Bread (page 149), Savory Brown Rice (page 212), and Cran-Applesauce (page 157).

MEATS

4 chicken breast halves

Herb Basting Sauce (recipe follows)

4 small tenderloin steaks (about 1½ pounds total)

¾ pound Italian or German sausages, fully cooked and left whole

VEGETABLES

1 red bell pepper, seeded and quartered

1 green bell pepper, seeded and quartered

1 red onion, sliced ½-inch thick

1 small eggplant, sliced lengthwise into ½-inch slices

1 zucchini, halved lengthwise

Prepare grill. Place chicken on a lightly oiled grill. Brush with basting sauce and grill 5 minutes, turning several times. Add steak and sausage to the grill and brush with basting sauce.

Arrange vegetables in an oil-sprayed, hinged wire rack, place on grill, and brush with basting sauce. Grill meats and vegetables about 10 minutes longer, turning several times.

Herb Basting Sauce

¼ cup vegetable oil

¼ cup balsamic vinegar,
   or red wine vinegar

2 cloves garlic, minced

1 tablespoon chopped
   fresh rosemary, or
   ½ teaspoon dried
   rosemary, crumbled

1 teaspoon chopped fresh
   oregano, or
   ½ teaspoon dried
   oregano, crumbled

½ teaspoon salt

In a small bowl or cup stir together
all ingredients.

Makes about ½ cup

Oriental Halibut Steaks

The addition of a marinade enhances the delicate flavor of halibut. Oriental Rice (page 211) is a natural to serve with this meal, along with California Salad with Tarragon-Sesame Seed Dressing (page 54) and Honey-Butter Carrots (page 168).

3 or 4 halibut steaks
  (1½ to 2 pounds)
Orange-Soy Marinade
  (recipe follows)

Place steaks in a 9- by 13-inch glass baking dish. Pour marinade over fish and marinate 30 minutes at room temperature. Turn several times.

Prepare grill. Remove halibut from marinade and place on a lightly oiled grill or in an oiled hinged wire grill-rack. Grill on one side for 4 to 5 minutes. Turn and brush with marinade. Broil until fish flakes when tested with a fork, 4 to 5 minutes longer.

Orange-Soy Marinade

¼ cup soy sauce
¼ cup orange juice
1 tablespoon vegetable
  oil
2 cloves garlic, minced
1 tablespoon fresh grated
  ginger, or ½ teaspoon
  ground ginger

In a bowl mix ingredients together.

Makes about ½ cup

Shrimp, Scallop, and Vegetable Kabobs

SERVES 6

A favorite entrée to serve with Caesar Salad, San Francisco Style (page 50), warm French bread, and Deep-dish Berry Pie (page 262) for dessert.

1 dozen large shrimp, peeled and deveined

1 dozen large scallops

Lemon-Herb Marinade (recipe follows)

1 small green or red bell pepper, cut into large pieces

1/2 pound mushroom caps

1 small yellow onion, cut into pieces

Rémoulade Sauce (page 111)

Place shrimp, scallops, and marinade in a bowl and toss. Let sit 15 minutes at room temperature.

Prepare grill. Remove shrimp and scallops from marinade and thread on skewers alternating with vegetables. Place skewers on a lightly oiled grill. Grill about 6 minutes on each side, turning often, and brushing with remaining marinade. Serve with Rémoulade Sauce.

Lemon-Herb Marinade

Juice of 1 lemon

2 tablespoons vegetable oil

1 clove garlic, minced

1 tablespoon chopped fresh basil, or 1 teaspoon dried basil, crumbled

1 tablespoon chopped fresh rosemary, or 1 teaspoon dried rosemary, crumbled

1 tablespoon chopped fresh thyme, or 1/4 teaspoon dried thyme, crumbled

1/2 teaspoon salt

Freshly ground pepper to taste

In a bowl mix all ingredients together.

Makes about 1/2 cup

Halibut with Yogurt-Cucumber-Dill Sauce

SERVES 4

Brush this simple baste on halibut, then grill to perfection.
For a carefree dinner, serve with Vegetable and Fresh Herb Casserole
(page 186), and frozen yogurt with Strawberry Sauce (page 288).

4 small halibut steaks
  (1½ to 2 pounds)
Lemon-Herb Marinade
  (page xx)
Yogurt-Cucumber-Dill
  Sauce (recipe follows)

Place steaks in a glass baking dish and marinate 15 minutes.

Prepare grill. Remove steaks from marinade and place in an oiled wire rack. Grill 5 minutes, turn, and brush with marinade. Grill until fish flakes when tested with a fork, about 5 minutes longer. Arrange fish on a warmed platter and serve immediately. Serve with Yogurt-Cucumber-Dill sauce in a separate bowl.

Yogurt-Cucumber-Dill Sauce

¾ cup plain nonfat yogurt
¼ cup light sour cream
1 small cucumber, seeded,
  chopped, and drained
  on a paper towel
2 green onions, sliced
1 clove garlic, minced
1 teaspoon lemon juice
½ teaspoon dry dill weed
¼ teaspoon salt

In a small bowl stir together all ingredients. Cover and refrigerate until ready to use. Serve at room temperature.

Makes 1¼ cups

Grilled Salmon Fillets with Fruit Kabobs

Here the salmon is grilled quickly to retain the wonderful fresh flavor. The Fruit Kabobs, along with Lemony Green Beans (page 166) and Wild Rice Plus (page 210) make an attractive presentation.

2 pounds salmon fillet (skin on), cut into serving pieces

Lemon-Herb Marinade (page 251)

Fruit Kabobs (recipe follows)

Place steaks in a glass dish and marinate 15 minutes.

Prepare grill. Place fish on a lightly oiled grill skin side down and grill with lid closed. Brush several times with marinade. Do not turn. Grill until fish flakes when tested with a fork, about 15 minutes. Arrange fish, skin removed, on a warmed platter and serve immediately with Fruit Kabobs.

Fruit Kabobs

Grilled fruit tinged with a light smoky flavor complements any fish.

½ cantaloupe, cut into 1-inch cubes

½ honeydew melon, cut into 1-inch cubes

1 cup 1-inch cubes watermelon

Balsamic vinegar, for brushing on fruit

Prepare grill. Alternate cubes of fruit on metal skewers or water-soaked wooden skewers. Brush with vinegar. Place on vegetable-oiled grill until fruit is warmed, about 5 minutes. Turn several times while cooking.

Serves 4

Grilled Corn on the Cob

Grilling corn brings out a sweet, smoky flavor and is fun to do while grilling meats.

4 ears of corn
1/4 teaspoon salt
Water to cover

Pull back husks and remove silk from corn. Fold husks back over corn and tie with twine. In a large pan soak corn in salted water for 1 hour.

Prepare grill. Remove corn from water and drain, shaking off excess water. Place on grill and grill until husks are charred and brown and kernels are bright yellow and tender, turning several times, about 15 minutes. Serve immediately.

Great Endings

Everyone looks forward to dessert and, for some, it is the highlight of the meal. From an elegant dinner to a casual get-together, homemade desserts make any occasion special.

Choose the right dessert to complement the meal. If the entrée is heavy and filling, the dessert should be light and refreshing; if the entrée is modest and light, a rich, more decadent dessert is appropriate. Because of calorie and cholesterol concerns, fresh fruit desserts have gained in popularity. They are easy to make and are satisfying as well as delicious.

Dessert Basics

Unlike other recipes, dessert recipes must be followed precisely, especially by the beginner.

Read the recipe carefully to be sure you have all the ingredients on hand. Assemble all the ingredients before starting.

Measure ingredients accurately. Level off dry ingredients with the straight edge of a knife.

Butter or unsalted butter is recommended for baking, especially pastry. Unsalted butter has a fresher taste, is creamier, and the amount of salt in the recipe can be more easily controlled. Without salt, butter is more perishable and must be used promptly or kept frozen. Margarine (stick only) or a combination of margarine and butter can be used for other baking with good results.

Flour is now presifted and does not need to be sifted again unless specified in the recipe. Use all-purpose flour unless otherwise specified.

Preheat the oven before baking. It is important to have an accurate oven temperature. Check with an oven thermometer.

Always use the size of the pan called for in the recipe.

Bake cookies on a parchment-lined baking sheet for even browning and easy clean up.

Chill bowl and beater when whipping cream.

Lightly flour work surface and hands when working with pastry.

Chocolate can be melted quickly in the microwave oven but must be watched carefully.

Fresh Peach Crisp

Make this wonderful crisp when peaches are at their peak. Serve with vanilla ice cream or frozen yogurt.

8 large ripe peaches, peeled, halved, pitted, and sliced (see note)
1/4 cup granulated sugar
1 teaspoon cornstarch
1/4 teaspoon salt
1 teaspoon fresh lemon juice

TOPPING
3/4 cup all-purpose flour
3/4 cup firmly packed brown sugar
1/2 cup butter or margarine
1/2 cup chopped walnuts

Whipped cream, vanilla ice cream, or frozen yogurt (optional)

Preheat oven to 375°F. Arrange peach slices in a lightly oiled or sprayed 8- by 8-inch baking dish. In a small bowl stir together granulated sugar, cornstarch, and salt, then stir into peaches along with lemon juice.

To make topping, in a food processor, combine flour, sugar, and butter. Using on-off pulses, process until crumbly or combine ingredients in a bowl and using a pastry blender cut in butter until crumbly. Mix in nuts. Sprinkle topping evenly over the peaches.

Bake until fruit is bubbly and topping is lightly browned, about 40 minutes. Cool on rack. Serve warm or at room temperature with topping of your choice.

Note: To peel peaches, drop into boiling water 10 to 20 seconds, drain, and slip off skins.

Spiced Apple Crisp

A change of season calls for this fall or winter dessert of apples and spices. Serve warm from the oven with vanilla ice cream and a wedge of sharp Cheddar cheese.

7 large cooking apples, such as Golden Delicious, peeled, cored, and sliced

2 tablespoons fresh lemon juice

1/3 cup granulated sugar

1/2 teaspoon ground cinnamon

1/4 teaspoon ground nutmeg

1/4 teaspoon ground cloves

1/4 teaspoon ground allspice

TOPPING

1/2 cup firmly packed brown sugar

3/4 cup all-purpose flour

1/4 teaspoon salt

6 tablespoons butter

1/2 cup chopped walnuts

Vanilla ice cream or frozen yogurt, for topping (optional)

Sharp Cheddar cheese slices (optional)

Preheat oven to 375°F. Place apples in a lightly oiled or sprayed 7½- by 11¾-inch baking dish. Stir in lemon juice. In a small bowl combine granulated sugar with spices and sprinkle over apples.

To make topping, in food processor combine all ingredients except nuts. Using on-off pulses, process until crumbly, or combine ingredients in a bowl and using a pastry blender cut in butter until crumbly. Stir in nuts and spread topping evenly over apples.

Bake until apple mixture is bubbly and topping is lightly browned, about 40 minutes. Cool on a rack. Serve warm or cold with ice cream or Cheddar cheese, if desired.

Blueberry–Cranberry Crisp

Berry desserts are always refreshing to serve, especially after a hearty meal. Keep blueberries and cranberries in the freezer for year-round use.

2 cups fresh or frozen
 blueberries
2 cups fresh or frozen
 cranberries
¾ cup granulated sugar
¼ cup all-purpose flour
2 tablespoons lemon juice
Dash of salt

TOPPING
½ cup all-purpose flour
¼ cup brown sugar
¼ teaspoon cinnamon
¼ cup butter, cut up
¼ cup rolled oats

Preheat oven to 350°F. In an 8- by 8-inch lightly oiled or sprayed baking dish, mix blueberries, cranberries, sugar, flour, lemon juice, and salt.

To make topping, in food processor combine topping ingredients and, using on-off pulses, process until crumbly or combine ingredients in a bowl and using a pastry blender, cut in butter until crumbly. Spread topping evenly over fruit.

Bake until fruit is bubbly and topping is lightly browned, about 35 minutes. Cool on a rack. Serve warm or at room temperature.

Blueberry Pie

Fresh, juicy blueberries capture the taste of summer in this easy pie. Serve with vanilla ice cream or frozen yogurt.

1 nine-inch Pie Shell (recipe follows), baked and cooled

4 cups blueberries, washed and drained well

1 cup granulated sugar

3 tablespoons cornstarch

¼ cup water

¼ teaspoon salt

1 tablespoon fresh lemon juice

1 tablespoon butter

Fill pie shell with 2 cups berries. In a saucepan over medium heat combine remaining 2 cups berries, sugar, cornstarch, water, salt, and lemon juice.

Bring to a boil over medium heat and cook, stirring constantly, until mixture thickens slightly and turns clear, 5 to 6 minutes. Remove from heat and stir in butter. Cool about 10 minutes, then pour mixture over berries in shell. Serve warm or chilled.

Pie Shell

1 ¼ cups all-purpose flour
½ teaspoon salt
6 tablespoons chilled
   butter, cut into small
   pieces
3 tablespoons chilled
   vegetable shortening
3 to 4 tablespoons
   ice water

In a food processor place all ingredients except water. With on-off pulses, process until mixture resembles coarse meal, about 30 times. With the motor running, slowly add water one table-spoon at a time until dough sticks together, before a ball forms (you may not need all the water). Turn dough onto a piece of waxed paper and flatten into a 6-inch disk. Wrap with waxed paper and chill 30 minutes.

Preheat oven to 475°F. On a lightly floured surface and with a floured rolling pin, roll dough from the center to the edges until pastry is 2 inches larger than pie plate. Fold pastry in half and place in pie plate. Unfold the other half and press firmly against bottom and sides. Trim overhanging edge 1 inch from rim of plate. Tuck under and crimp edge With a fork prick bottom and sides thoroughly to prevent crust from puffing.

Bake until light brown, 8 to 10 minutes. Cool on a wire rack, then fill.

Makes 1 nine- or ten-inch pie shell

Deep-dish Berry Pie

Enjoy the endless pleasure of mixed berries topped with a flaky crust. This is a perfect summer dessert for a barbecue or picnic. Serve with vanilla ice cream or frozen yogurt.

5 cups mixed berries (blueberries, blackberries, or
   marionberries)
2/3 cup sugar
1/4 cup tapioca
1 tablespoon fresh lemon
   juice

Pastry for 1 nine- or ten-inch Pie Shell (page 261), rolled out but unbaked.

Preheat oven to 425°F. In a 10- by 2-inch deep-dish pie plate mix all ingredients. Cover fruit with pastry; fold the edge under and crimp the edges to seal tightly against dish. With a sharp knife cut several small slits in top of pastry to allow steam to escape. Cover the edge with a 2-inch strip of aluminum foil to prevent overbrowning.

Bake pie for 10 minutes, remove foil, reduce temperature to 350°F, and bake until crust is golden and juices are bubbling out of slits, 35 to 40 minutes longer. Cool on a wire rack.

Rhubarb Crumble

The tart flavor and rosy hue of rhubarb make an appealing as well as tasty dessert.

6 cups 1-inch slices rhubarb (about 2 pounds)
1 cup granulated sugar

TOPPING
1 cup all-purpose flour
¼ cup granulated sugar
¼ teaspoon ground cinnamon
⅛ teaspoon salt
6 tablespoons butter, at room temperature

Vanilla ice cream or frozen yogurt

Preheat oven to 350°F. In a lightly sprayed 8- by 8-inch baking dish, combine rhubarb and 1 cup sugar.

To make topping, in food processor combine all ingredients. Using on-off pulses, process until crumbly or combine all ingredients in a bowl, and using a pastry blender, cut in butter until crumbly. Sprinkle topping evenly over rhubarb.

Bake until juices are bubbly and topping is slightly browned, about 45 minutes. Serve warm or at room temperature with ice cream.

Sour Cream Lemon Pie

Be ready to serve seconds of this rich, luscious pie with a velvety, sweet-tart filling.

1 cup milk
1 egg
1 egg yolk
1 cup granulated sugar
¼ cup cornstarch
¼ cup butter, cut up
Juice of 1 lemon (about ¼ cup)
1 tablespoon grated lemon zest (see note)
1 cup light sour cream
Graham Cracker Crust, baked (page 268) (omit nuts), or 1 nine- or ten-inch Pie Shell (page 261), baked
Whipped Cream (page 273) (optional)

In a small bowl whisk together milk, egg, and egg yolk. In a saucepan over medium heat mix sugar, cornstarch, butter, lemon juice, lemon zest, and milk-egg mixture. Stir constantly until thickened, 10 to 12 minutes.

Cover pan with waxed paper and cool in refrigerator about 1 hour. Stir in sour cream and pour into baked shell. Cover lightly and chill 4 to 6 hours before serving. Serve with Whipped Cream, if desired.

Note: Zest is the outermost colored part of the citrus peel. When added to a recipe, it intensifies the flavor. If you don't have a zesting tool, you may use a fine grater. Do not include the bitter white part of the peel.

Chocolate Fudge Pie with Hazelnut Whipped Cream

SERVES 6

Everyone likes a chocolate dessert, and here is one that will become one of your favorites for family or friends.

2 eggs
1 cup granulated sugar
1/4 cup all-purpose flour
Dash of salt
1/2 cup butter
2 squares (1 ounce each)
    unsweetened chocolate
1 teaspoon vanilla
1 unbaked 9-inch pie
    shell (page 261)
1/2 cup chopped toasted
    hazelnuts
Hazelnut Whipped Cream
    (recipe follows)

Preheat oven to 350°F. In a bowl and using an electric mixer, beat eggs and sugar together. Add flour and salt and beat until well mixed.

In a saucepan over low heat melt butter and chocolate. Add vanilla. Add to flour mixture and beat well. Pour into pie shell and sprinkle with nuts. Bake until a toothpick inserted in the center comes out clean, about 35 minutes. Cool on a rack. Serve with Hazelnut Whipped Cream.

Hazelnut Whipped Cream

1 tablespoon brown
    sugar, packed
1 tablespoon hazelnut
    liqueur
1 cup whipping cream

In a small bowl stir together sugar and liqueur until sugar is dissolved. Stir in whipping cream and using an electric mixer, beat until stiff peaks form, 5 to 6 minutes.

Makes about 2 cups

Flan (Crème Caramel)

A simple yet elegant finale. When this velvety custard is unmolded, the caramel glaze forms a sauce on top and around it.

¾ cup granulated sugar
3 large eggs
2 cups half-and-half or
    whole milk
1 teaspoon vanilla extract

Preheat oven to 325°F. In a heavy skillet over high heat stir ½ cup sugar with a wooden spoon constantly until sugar melts and turns amber in color, about 3 minutes. Quickly pour out sugar mixture, dividing equally among 6 custard cups, and arrange cups in a baking pan.

In a bowl whisk eggs with remaining ¼ cup sugar. Whisk in half-and-half and vanilla. Pour into prepared custard cups. Pour hot tap water into baking pan to come halfway up on cups.

Bake until a knife inserted in the center comes out clean, 45 to 50 minutes. Remove cups from pan and cool; then cover and refrigerate.

To serve, run a knife around custard and invert onto a dessert plate.

Apricot and Blueberry Flan

SERVES 8

A delicious, rich, elegant dessert to make for company. Serve with whipped cream or ice cream, if desired, but it is just as good without.

1/2 cup butter, cut up
3/4 cup sugar
1 1/3 cup all-purpose flour
1/2 teaspoon salt
1/4 teaspoon baking powder
1 teaspoon cinnamon
2 cans (16 ounces each) apricot halves, drained
1 cup blueberries (fresh or frozen), rinsed and drained
1 cup light cream (half-and-half)
1 egg
Whipped cream or vanilla ice cream

Preheat oven to 375°F. In food processor mix butter, sugar, flour, salt, baking powder, and cinnamon until fine. Reserve 1/3 cup for topping and set aside.

Using a 10-inch flan pan with removable bottom, press remaining mixture into pan and up the sides. Place apricot halves, cut-side up, evenly on the crust. Scatter blueberries over. Sprinkle on reserved topping. Bake 20 minutes.

In a pitcher or bowl whisk cream with egg. Pour mixture over flan while still in the oven. Bake until set, 25 minutes longer. Cool on a wire rack. Remove rim from pan and cut flan into wedges. Top with whipped cream or ice cream.

Hazelnut Cheesecake

This is a smaller, lighter cheesecake with a hazelnut accent. It should be made a day ahead to allow flavors to develop.

GRAHAM CRACKER-
HAZELNUT CRUST

1 1/2 cups graham cracker crumbs, about 20 squares, broken up

1/4 cup toasted hazelnuts (page 58)

2 tablespoons firmly packed brown sugar

1/3 cup butter, melted

FILLING

12 ounces cream cheese, at room temperature, cut up

3/4 cup granulated sugar

2 tablespoons hazelnut liqueur

2 eggs

TOPPING

1 cup light sour cream

2 tablespoons granulated sugar

1 teaspoon hazelnut liqueur

To make crust, in food processor process crackers, nuts, and sugar until mixture is fine. With motor running, add butter through the tube. Process until mixture is blended. Transfer to a 9-inch pie plate and with fingers press against the bottom and sides of plate. Refrigerate 10 minutes while making filling. (If using pie shell for other fillings, bake shell 10 minutes at 350°F.) Preheat oven to 350°F.

To make filling, in food processor combine all filling ingredients. Process until well blended, about 1 minute. Scrape down filling in food processor with a spatula to aid in mixing. Turn mixture into uncooked crust. Bake until filling is set, about 30 minutes.

To make topping, in a small bowl stir together all ingredients and set aside. Remove cheesecake from oven and spread topping over. Return to oven and bake 10 minutes longer. Cool on wire rack. When cool, cover and refrigerate at least 4 hours or overnight. Cut into wedges for serving.

Fresh Pear–Walnut Torte

Winter pears along with walnuts team together for this delicious cake-like dessert. If pears are not in season, canned pears may be used. Serve with vanilla ice cream or frozen yogurt.

2 eggs
1 1/2 cups granulated sugar
1 teaspoon vanilla
1 cup chopped walnuts
2 fresh pears, peeled, cored, and chopped (about 1 to 1 1/2 cups), or canned pears, drained
1/2 cup all-purpose flour
1/4 teaspoon salt
2 teaspoons baking powder
Vanilla ice cream or frozen yogurt

Preheat oven to 350°F. In a bowl beat eggs, sugar, and vanilla with an electric mixer until light. Fold in nuts and pears. On a piece of waxed paper mix flour, salt, and baking powder and stir into batter. Pour into a lightly oiled or sprayed 8- by 8-inch baking dish.

Bake until a toothpick inserted in the center comes out clean, about 35 minutes. Cool on a rack. Cut into squares and top with ice cream or frozen yogurt.

Kahlúa Chocolate Ice Cream Torte

This dessert is done in stages and takes about eight or nine hours (off and on) to prepare, but it is not complicated. It makes a great company dessert because it is made ahead and will generously serve eight.

½ cup butter

½ cup chopped walnuts or almonds

1 cup all-purpose flour

½ cup granulated sugar

1 cup whipping cream, whipped

¼ cup coffee-flavored liqueur (Kahlúa or Kamora)

2 tablespoons strong coffee

1 quart chocolate ice cream, slightly softened

In a large skillet over medium heat melt butter. Add nuts, flour, and sugar and stir constantly, breaking up with a wooden spoon, until mixture is golden and crumbly, about 8 minutes. Raise temperature to medium-high the last few minutes to achieve a golden color if necessary. Measure out ¾ cup of mixture for topping and set aside. Press remaining mixture onto the bottom of a 9-inch springform pan. Cover and freeze for 4 hours.

In a bowl combine whipped cream, liqueur, coffee, and ice cream and with an electric mixer beat until smooth. Spoon into prepared pan. Freeze until almost set, about 2 hours. Sprinkle with reserved crumb mixture, cover and return to freezer and freeze until firm, 2 to 3 hours or overnight.

To serve, release springform pan and transfer to a decorative plate or cake stand. Cut into wedges.

Filled Pumpkin Dessert

Here is a dessert that is fun to serve during the Halloween season.
It is so easy, kids can make it.

1 small pumpkin (about
   8 inches in diameter)
2/3 cup firmly packed
   brown sugar
1/2 cup butter, melted
3 small apples, peeled
   and thinly sliced
1 cup golden raisins
1/2 cup chopped walnuts
1/4 teaspoon cinnamon
Dash of ground nutmeg

Vanilla ice cream or
   frozen yogurt

Preheat oven to 350°F. Cut top off pumpkin to make a lid and remove and discard strings and seeds (as if making a jack-o-lantern). Fill pumpkin with remaining ingredients. Place pumpkin in a pie plate. Place top back on pumpkin.

Bake until pumpkin is slightly browned and begins to lose its shape, about 1½ hours. Cool slightly. Arrange on a plate decorated with fall leaves and chrysanthemums and serve at the table.

Scoop out the filling, along with some of the pumpkin pulp, into dessert bowls and top with ice cream. Serve warm or at room temperature.

Fruit Trifle

Originating in England, but served in many countries, this dessert layered with pudding, cake, and fruit makes an appealing and tempting presentation.

1 sixteen-ounce sponge or pound cake (purchased or homemade), cut into ½-inch slices and halved

¼ cup cream sherry or rum

2¼ cups sliced strawberries or 2 cups blueberries (reserve 10 strawberry slices or 10 blueberries for garnish)

2 kiwis, peeled and sliced

2 bananas, peeled and sliced

Vanilla Pudding (recipe follows), or 1 package (3.1 ounces) vanilla pudding

Whipped Cream (recipe follows)

Mint leaves, for garnish

Brush cake slices with sherry or rum. Arrange half the slices on the bottom of an 8- by 4-inch straight-sided glass bowl. Attractively arrange a layer of half the fruit on top. Spoon half the vanilla pudding over. Repeat another layer with remaining ingredients.

Cover and chill several hours. Top with Whipped Cream and garnish with reserved strawberry slices and mint leaves just before serving. Serve at the table in dessert dishes.

Vanilla Pudding

2 egg yolks
1/3 cup sugar
2 tablespoons cornstarch
1/8 teaspoon salt
2 cups milk
2 tablespoons butter,
    at room temperature
1 teaspoon vanilla extract

In a small bowl lightly beat egg yolks and set aside. In a saucepan stir together sugar, cornstarch, salt, and milk. Place over medium heat, stirring constantly, until mixture comes to a boil and thickens slightly. Stir and boil 1 minute. Gradually stir half of the mixture into egg yolks. Return egg yolk mixture to the pan. Boil 1 minute longer, stirring constantly. Remove from heat and whisk in butter and vanilla. Lightly cover with waxed paper and cool until ready to use.

Makes about 2 cups

Whipped Cream

1 cup whipping cream
2 tablespoons powdered
    sugar

In a bowl with an electric mixer beat cream until stiff peaks form. Beat in powdered sugar.

Strawberry Shortcake

Make this all-American favorite when local berries are available from the field in late spring and early summer. Juicy strawberries and tender Sweet Buttermilk Biscuits topped with Lemon Whipped Cream are an unbeatable combination.

4 cups strawberries, lightly rinsed, hulled, and sliced

2 to 3 tablespoons sugar

Sweet Buttermilk Biscuits (recipe follows)

Lemon Whipped Cream (recipe follows) or vanilla ice cream

In a bowl stir together berries and sugar and let stand about 1 hour, stirring occasionally.

To serve, cut the biscuits in half horizontally and place one half on a plate. Add a large spoonful of berries and a dollop of Lemon Whipped Cream (or vanilla ice cream), then top with remaining biscuit half and add more berries and whipped cream on top. Serve immediately.

Sweet Buttermilk Biscuits

2 cups all-purpose flour
1/3 cup sugar
1/2 teaspoon baking soda
2 teaspoons baking powder
1/2 teaspoon salt
1/2 cup butter or margarine, cut into chunks
3/4 cup buttermilk

Preheat oven to 400°F. In a large bowl combine flour, sugar, baking soda, baking powder, and salt. Add butter and, with pastry blender, cut in butter until mixture looks like coarse crumbs. With a fork stir in milk until dough sticks together. Gather into a ball and transfer to a lightly floured surface. With floured hands, knead dough until smooth, about 10 turns. Reflour board and pat out dough to 1/2 inch thick. Cut into circles with a 2½- to 3-inch round cutter. Shape scraps together to make more rounds. Place 1 inch apart on an ungreased baking sheet. Bake until golden and puffed, 12 to 14 minutes. Transfer to a rack to cool.

Makes about 10 biscuits

Lemon Whipped Cream

2 cups whipping cream
1 teaspoon lemon zest
2 tablespoons sugar

In a small bowl with electric mixer whip cream until peaks form. Fold in zest and sugar.

Makes about 4 cups

Citrus–Nut Cake

Make this cake at least one day before serving. It is ideal as dessert with vanilla ice cream or frozen yogurt or just plain as a breakfast or luncheon bread.

3 cups all-purpose flour
1 teaspoon baking
    powder
1 teaspoon baking soda
1/4 teaspoon salt
1 cup coarsely chopped
    walnuts or other nuts
1 cup butter, at room
    temperature
1 1/4 cups granulated
    sugar
3 eggs
1 1/4 cups buttermilk
1 tablespoon lemon zest
    (page 264)
1 tablespoon orange zest
Citrus Topping (recipe
    follows)
Candied orange slices, for
    garnish (optional)

Preheat oven to 350°F. In a bowl combine flour, baking powder, baking soda, salt, and nuts. Set aside.

In another bowl, with an electric mixer, cream butter with sugar. Add eggs one at a time, beating well after each addition. Stir in flour mixture, alternating with buttermilk. Add zests and mix well. Pour into an oiled and floured Bundt pan. Bake until toothpick inserted in center comes out clean, about 1 hour.

Remove pan to a rack. With a skewer prick hot cake at 1-inch intervals and slowly pour citrus topping over. Cool cake in pan and then remove from pan and wrap in airtight wrap. Serve with candied orange slices.

Citrus Topping

½ cup granulated sugar
Juice of 1 orange
Juice of 1 lemon

In a cup or small bowl stir together sugar and juices until sugar is dissolved.

Makes about ¾ cup

Buttermilk Chocolate Cake

Need a cake for a crowd? This is an all-time favorite.

1 cup water
1 cup butter, cut into pieces
¼ cup cocoa
2 cups all-purpose flour
2 cups granulated sugar
1 teaspoon baking soda
½ teaspoon cinnamon
2 eggs
½ cup buttermilk
1 teaspoon vanilla
Cocoa Frosting (recipe follows)

Preheat oven to 350°F. In a small saucepan over medium heat bring water, butter, and cocoa to a boil. Stir until blended and set aside.

In a bowl stir together flour, sugar, baking soda, and cinnamon. Pour cocoa mixture into flour mixture and beat until smooth. Beat in eggs and buttermilk. Add vanilla and mix well. Pour batter into a lightly buttered 12- by 15½- by 1½-inch jelly-roll pan.

Bake until a toothpick inserted into the center of cake comes out clean, about 30 minutes. Cool cake on a rack and frost.

Cocoa Frosting

½ cup butter, cut into pieces
¼ cup cocoa
¼ cup buttermilk
1 pound powdered sugar
1 teaspoon vanilla extract
1 cup chopped walnuts

In a saucepan over medium heat stir butter, cocoa, and buttermilk until butter is melted and ingredients are hot and blended. Remove from heat and add powdered sugar and vanilla. Beat with electric mixer until frosting is smooth. Spread over cake and sprinkle with walnuts.

Frosts a 12- by 15-inch cake or two 8- or 9-inch cake layers

Grandma's Coffee Crumb Cake

Make this tender, moist cake a day before serving. It will become a family favorite for brunch or afternoon coffee.

2¼ cups all-purpose flour

¼ teaspoon salt

2 teaspoons ground cinnamon

1 cup firmly packed brown sugar

¾ cup granulated sugar

¾ cup vegetable oil

1 cup chopped pecans or walnuts

1 teaspoon baking powder

1 teaspoon baking soda

¼ teaspoon ground nutmeg

1 egg

1 cup buttermilk

Preheat oven to 325°F. In a bowl place flour, salt, 1 teaspoon cinnamon, sugars, and oil. Beat with an electric mixer until evenly blended. Transfer ¾ cup for topping to a small bowl, stir in nuts, and set aside.

To remaining mixture, add baking powder, baking soda, remaining 1 teaspoon cinnamon, nutmeg, egg, and buttermilk and beat until smooth. Turn batter into a 9- by 13-inch lightly oiled or sprayed baking dish. Sprinkle reserved topping over batter and lightly pat down with the back of a spoon. Bake until a toothpick inserted in center comes out clean, 35 to 40 minutes. Cool on a wire rack and cut into squares.

Note: To warm, cover and place in a microwave oven for about 30 seconds.

Cashew Brownies

No need to use a mix when you can make these delicious, light, chewy brownies just about as fast. They are delicious served warm or at room temperature. Cocoa packs a lot of chocolate flavor, but has less fat than solid chocolate. For a fancier dessert, serve with warm caramel sauce and vanilla ice cream.

1 cup butter
1/4 cup cocoa
2 cups granulated sugar
3 eggs
1 cup all-purpose flour
1/4 teaspoon baking powder
1 teaspoon vanilla
1/2 cup coarsely chopped unsalted cashew nuts or walnuts

Preheat oven to 350°F. In a saucepan over medium heat melt butter. Add cocoa and mix well. Add sugar and stir until sugar is dissolved and blended. Transfer to a bowl. Add eggs, one at a time and, with an electric mixer, beat well after each addition. Beat in flour, baking powder, and vanilla. Fold in nuts and pour into a lightly oiled or sprayed 7½- by 11¾-inch baking dish. Bake until toothpick comes out clean when tested in the center, 35 to 40 minutes.

Remove from oven and let stand on rack 10 minutes; then cut into 2-inch squares. Remove from pan while warm and place on a rack to cool. Do not leave in pan. To store for several days, wrap in foil.

Old-fashioned Icebox Cookies

Stir up a few childhood memories by serving these cookies warm from the oven with a glass of milk. The dough needs to be made and frozen a day in advance for easy slicing. These are good cookies to keep on hand for unexpected guests.

1 cup butter, at room temperature
1 cup margarine, at room temperature
1 cup granulated sugar
1 cup firmly packed brown sugar
3 eggs
4 cups all-purpose flour
1/2 teaspoon salt
1 cup chopped walnuts
1 teaspoon vanilla extract

In a large bowl, cream together butter, margarine, and sugars until fluffy. Add eggs one at a time, beating well after each addition. Stir in flour, salt, nuts, and vanilla, and mix well. (It takes a long time.) The dough will be soft and sticky.

Divide dough into 3 equal portions and place each portion onto a 12- by 14-inch piece of waxed paper. (For easier handling, chill dough 15 minutes in the refrigerator before making logs.) With wet hands, form each portion into a 10- by 2-inch log. Flatten top of each roll, wrap in waxed paper, and freeze overnight.

Preheat oven to 400°F. Remove logs from freezer and let stand 10 minutes before slicing. Cut into slices 1/4-inch thick and arrange on an ungreased baking sheet, 1/2 inch apart. Bake until lightly browned, 10 to 12 minutes. Cool on a wire rack. Store in airtight container.

Note: Frozen dough logs keep for 3 to 4 weeks.

Lemon Drop Cookies

These cakelike cookies go well with fresh fruit. The frosting makes them special.

½ cup butter or
    margarine
1½ cups granulated sugar
2 eggs
2⅔ cups all-purpose flour
½ teaspoon baking
    powder
1 teaspoon baking soda
½ teaspoon salt
1 cup light sour cream
1 teaspoon lemon zest
1 tablespoon lemon juice
Lemon Frosting
    (recipe follows)

Preheat oven to 375°F. In a large bowl and using an electric mixer, cream together butter and sugar until fluffy. Beat in eggs, one at a time. In another bowl or on a large piece of waxed paper, mix together flour, baking powder, baking soda, and salt. One-third at a time and beating well after each addition, add flour mixture to egg mixture, alternating with sour cream. Stir in lemon zest and lemon juice. Drop by teaspoonfuls, 1½ inches apart, onto parchment-lined baking sheet.

Bake until lightly browned, about 10 minutes. Remove and cool on a wire rack. Frost with Lemon Frosting.

Lemon Frosting

6 tablespoons butter
2½ cups powdered sugar
1 tablespoon lemon juice
½ teaspoon vanilla
Few drops water

In a saucepan melt butter. Stir in sugar, lemon juice, and vanilla. Add enough water to create a good spreading consistency.

Makes enough frosting for 4 dozen cookies

Frosted Chocolate Cookies

Cocoa is used instead of chocolate for a cookie that is lighter than most but just as delicious. The frosting makes the cookies even better.

1 cup granulated sugar
3/4 cup butter, melted
1 egg
6 tablespoons cocoa
1/2 cup low-fat milk
1 teaspoon vanilla extract
2 cups all-purpose flour
1/2 teaspoon baking soda
1/2 teaspoon salt
1 cup chopped walnuts or other nuts

Chocolate Frosting
(recipe follows)

Preheat oven to 375°F. In a bowl mix sugar, butter, egg, cocoa, milk, and vanilla. Stir in remaining ingredients. Drop dough by rounded teaspoonfuls 2 inches apart on a parchment-lined baking sheet. Bake until firm, 8 to 10 minutes. Remove and cool on a rack. Frost with Chocolate Frosting.

Chocolate Frosting

2 tablespoons butter
About 2 tablespoons low-fat milk
3 tablespoons cocoa
2 cups powdered sugar
1 teaspoon vanilla

In a small saucepan over medium heat melt butter with milk. Remove from heat. Stir in cocoa and sugar and beat until smooth. Add more milk if needed for spreading consistency. Stir in vanilla.

Makes enough frosting for 4 dozen cookies

Toffee Nut Bars

These bars with an almond-coconut layer go together in two easy steps. They are as good as they look.

FIRST LAYER

1/2 cup butter

1/2 cup firmly packed
   brown sugar

1 cup all-purpose flour

SECOND LAYER

2 eggs

1 cup firmly packed
   brown sugar

1 teaspoon vanilla

2 tablespoons all-purpose
   flour

1 teaspoon baking
   powder

1/4 teaspoon salt

1 cup shredded coconut

1 cup chopped almonds

To prepare the first layer, preheat oven to 350°F. In a bowl and with an electric mixer, cream butter and sugar together. Stir in flour until crumbly. Press mixture into lightly oiled or sprayed 7 1/2- by 11 3/4-inch baking dish. Bake 10 minutes.

Meanwhile, assemble ingredients for second layer.

In a bowl and with an electric mixer beat eggs, sugar, and vanilla. Beat in flour, baking powder, and salt. Stir in coconut and almonds.

Remove dish from oven and spread second layer on top and bake until golden, 25 minutes longer. Cool on a wire rack, then cut into bars.

Cranberry Sorbet

In recent years, fruit sorbets have been appearing on dessert menus in chic restaurants. Two sorbets are often paired together. Team this one with Fresh Pear Sorbet (page 286).

1 package (12 ounces) fresh or frozen cranberries, washed and sorted

1½ cups sugar

1 cup water

1 tablespoon crème de cassis liqueur (optional)

1 tablespoon orange juice

1 cup ginger ale or water

In a saucepan over medium-high heat stir together cranberries, sugar, and water and bring to a boil. Cook until berries begin to pop, about 3 minutes, stirring occasionally.

Transfer to food processor or blender and purée until smooth. Transfer to a sieve over a deep bowl and with the back of a spoon press mixture through sieve. Add remaining ingredients and mix well. Freeze in an electric ice-cream maker according to manufacturer's directions. Let stand for several hours in maker before serving or transfer to another container and place in freezer. Remove from freezer 10 minutes before serving.

Note: To make sorbet without an electric ice-cream maker, spread the mixture into a 9- by 13-inch glass baking dish, cover, and freeze until firm, about 3 hours. Remove from freezer and stir with a spoon, breaking up mixture, or transfer to food processor and process until blended. Return to dish and refreeze for several hours. Remove from freezer 10 minutes before serving.

Fresh Pear Sorbet

Sorbets can be served before the main course to clear and stimulate the palate or as a refreshing dessert. Serve with Old-fashioned Icebox Cookies (page 281).

1 cup water

1 cup sugar

3 large fresh, ripe pears, peeled, cored, and cut into chunks

1 tablespoon lemon juice

1/4 teaspoon ground ginger

2 tablespoons Triple Sec liqueur or orange juice

In a small saucepan stir water and sugar together. Bring to a boil and stir until sugar is completely dissolved. Remove from heat and chill in refrigerator for 1 hour.

Place pears in food processor or blender and purée. Stir into sugar syrup and add remaining ingredients. Freeze in an electric ice cream maker according to manufacturer's directions or in a dish in the freezer (see page 285). Let stand for several hours in maker before serving or transfer to another container and place in freezer. Remove from freezer 10 minutes before serving.

All-Purpose Berry Sauces

EACH MAKES ABOUT 2 CUPS

This sauce, which can be made year round with fresh or frozen blueberries, is good on ice cream, plain cake, or pancakes and waffles.

Blueberry Sauce

2 cups blueberries
1/4 cup granulated sugar
1/4 cup water
1/2 teaspoon lemon zest
2 teaspoons cornstarch

In a saucepan combine all ingredients. Cook over medium heat, stirring constantly, until slightly thickened, 3 to 4 minutes. Let cool to room temperature, then cover and refrigerate. Serve at room temperature.

Strawberry Sauce

In this recipe both fresh and frozen berries are combined for a really fresh flavor. This, too, is good on ice cream, plain cake, or pancakes and waffles.

1 package (10 ounces) frozen strawberries, thawed
2 tablespoons granulated sugar
1 tablespoon cornstarch
1/4 cup orange juice
1 1/4 cups sliced fresh strawberries
1 tablespoon Grand Marnier liqueur (optional)

In food processor briefly purée frozen berries with their juice. Transfer to a pan. Add sugar, cornstarch, and orange juice and bring to a boil over medium-high heat, stirring constantly, until thickened, about 4 minutes. Remove from heat and add fresh berries and liqueur (if using). Let cool at room temperature, then cover and refrigerate. Serve at room temperature.

Table of Equivalents

The exact equivalents in the following tables have been rounded for convenience.

US/UK

oz=ounce
lb=pound
in=inch
ft=foot
tbl=tablespoon
fl oz=fluid ounce
qt=quart

Metric

g=gram
kg=kilogram
mm=millimeter
cm=centimeter
ml=milliliter
l=liter

Oven Temperatures

Fahrenheit	Celsius	Gas
250	120	1/2
275	140	1
300	150	2
325	160	3
350	180	4
375	190	5
400	200	6
425	220	7
450	230	8
475	240	9
500	260	10

Weights

US/UK	Metric
1 oz	30 g
2 oz	60 g
3 oz	90 g
4 oz (1/4 lb)	125 g
5 oz (1/3 lb)	155 g
6 oz	185 g
7 oz	220 g
8 oz (1/2 lb)	250 g
10 oz	315 g
12 oz (3/4 lb)	375 g
14 oz	440 g
16 oz (1 lb)	500 g
1 1/2 lb	750 g
2 lb	1 kg
3 lb	1.5 kg

Liquids

US	Metric	UK
2 tbl	30 ml	1 fl oz
1/4 cup	60 ml	2 fl oz
1/3 cup	80 ml	3 fl oz
1/2 cup	125 ml	4 fl oz
2/3 cup	160 ml	5 fl oz
3/4 cup	180 ml	6 fl oz
1 cup	250 ml	8 fl oz
1 1/2 cups	375 ml	12 fl oz
2 cups	500 ml	16 fl oz
4 cups/1 qt	1 l	32 fl oz

Length Measures

1/8 in	3 mm
1/4 in	6 mm
1/2 in	12 mm
1 in	2.5 cm
2 in	5 cm
3 in	7.5 cm
4 in	10 cm
5 in	13 cm
6 in	15 cm
7 in	18 cm
8 in	20 cm
9 in	23 cm
10 in	25 cm
11 in	28 cm
12in/1 ft	30 cm